MASS COMMUNICATION

MASS COMMUNICATION

Television, Radio, Film, Press

THE MEDIA AND THEIR PRACTICE IN THE UNITED STATES OF AMERICA

By ERIK BARNOUW

Associate Professor of Dramatic Arts in charge of
courses in television, radio, motion pictures
Columbia University
Editor, Center for Mass Communication
Columbia University Press

RINEHART & COMPANY, INC. *New York Toronto*

Published simultaneously in Canada by
Clarke, Irwin & Company, Ltd., Toronto

© 1956 by Erik Barnouw
Manufactured in the United States of America
Library of Congress Catalog Card Number: 56-7260

For S.B.

ACKNOWLEDGMENTS

Because the world of the mass media is so broad and varied, the author has needed many kinds of advice and help. He wishes especially to express gratitude to Joseph E. Barmack, Lyman Bryson, Marguerite Cannavaro, H. William Fitelson, Maury Glaubman, Edward Greif, Paul Harvey, Margery Johnston, Wallace Kendall, Edward King, Donald Langer, Abe Liss, Milton Mazer, M.D., Patrick E. McCaughey, James Nelson, Dorothy Oshlag, T. Lefoy Richman, Leo Seltzer, Roy Swift, G. D. Wiebe and Morton Wishengrad.

E.B.

CONTENTS

The HISTORY
of mass communication . . .

TO Americans who are seldom out of reach of a radio, seldom go a day without seeing a television program, seldom sit in a chair without finding a magazine, newspaper, comic book or pocket book at hand, seldom go from one place to another without getting advice from billboard, car card or loudspeaker, seldom go a week without seeing a movie at a theater, school, club, church or office—to people who are surrounded by these influences and take them for granted it may be difficult to think of them as representing a revolution. Yet they are a revolution in men's ways of disseminating information and ideas.

It has been called the *communications revolution*.

The devices that made it possible had their roots in centuries long gone. At first they developed slowly. But during the nineteenth and twentieth centuries their development, suddenly speeded by social change, has surged forward like a series of rocket explosions. These explosions comprise our communications revolution, which is a part of the Industrial Revolution.

To see clearly its scope and meaning, let us review it rapidly.

BEFORE IT ALL BEGAN. When the thirteen colonies declared their independence in 1776, the people got the news largely by word of mouth. Most people could not read. The streams of talk were fed by a trickle of printed matter, produced for the few who could read. There were newspapers, pamphlets, broadsides, books. The newspapers were read aloud in the coffeehouses.

Perhaps it is misleading to call them *newspapers*. Most

3

were dingy, four-page newsletters, issued weekly or irregularly.

Such a newsletter had generally started as the enterprise of one man, a printer. With a wooden hand press, some type and paper, he was ready for publication. He might get a mechanic or two to help him.

Of the approximately thirty-five such sheets in existence at the time of the Declaration of Independence, none employed anyone we would call a reporter. The idea of going out to look for news had not yet entered the newspaper field. The main contents of the papers were reader contributions— essays, letters. These made the newspaper a kind of forum. They might be vitriolic arguments or learned discussions on any subject considered of public interest.

A newspaper might also contain: brief items cribbed from other papers, often months old; news and rumor relayed by travelers, summarized by the printer; a few advertisements, many of them want ads.

With these modest offerings a printer-publisher of the 1770's or 1780's might serve a total of perhaps five hundred to eight hundred subscribers.

Even if he could have sold more copies, he might not have been able to print them. He had to set all type by hand. Each piece of paper had to be carefully laid in position by hand.

Even if he could have printed more, he might not have been able to get the paper. All paper was handmade. Most of it was imported. The rest was made, from rags, in a few dozen small paper mills struggling into existence in the colonies. Such a paper "manufactory" generally consisted of the proprietor and one or two helpers. These paper mills were constantly short of rags.

In printing methods and materials, there had been little

change since Johann Gutenberg in 1456 printed the Bible in movable type.

But there had been little reason for change. Soon there would be.

1 The Paper Tide

For the new nation, independence brought a great release of energy. New industries, discouraged under colonial rule, sprang up in the colonies. Growing markets invited rapid expansion of industries. New inventions made the expansion possible.

At the same time, ideas were boiling. The American and French Revolutions had weakened class barriers. In America the rising class of artisans and mechanics saw a boundless future before them. There was talk of votes for everyone, education for everyone. The artisans and mechanics felt a new dignity and importance.

In the 1830's, in Massachusetts, the first state-wide public-school system was started. In the 1830's also, trade unions were being formed.

In 1833 a twenty-three-year-old job printer, Benjamin Day, decided to start a new paper in New York City. He decided to aim his paper, the *Sun,* at the rising class of artisans and mechanics—a group never before thought of as patrons of the press. In all this Benjamin Day expressed the spirit of his times.

To win this new market, Day took a radical step. He decided to sell the *Sun* at one cent per copy. Most papers sold at six cents.

Day also took the radical step of hiring a fellow printer,

at four dollars per week, to attend police-court trials and write about them for the *Sun*. The reporter was entering American journalism.

This reporter described the shocking events in a humorous tone, in imitation of a successful English paper. The style was a sensation in New York. The *Sun* titillated and shocked its readers, while admonishing them against the evils of the day. Thus crime exposure became a feature of American journalism.

Day took another radical step. Always before, newspapers had been sold by subscription. Day sold the *Sun* at sixty-seven cents per hundred copies to newsboys. These boys, initiating a new form of competitive enterprise, swarmed into the streets to shout the horrifying and triumphant headlines. Promotion entered American journalism. The search for news, sensational content, aggressive promotion—this combination made history.

The *Sun* started with an old-style hand press that could turn out two hundred copies per hour, one side at a time. This wasn't enough. In his second year, 1834, Day bought a new kind of press, a cylinder press that could print both sides at a time. It was fed a new kind of paper, machine-made in continuous rolls. Now Day could print two thousand copies per hour. It still wasn't enough. In England the presses of the London *Times* were being driven by steam. In 1835, Day acquired a steam press. That year the paid circulation of the *Sun* reached twenty thousand—largest in the world.

In that same year the New York *Herald* was started, also at one cent. It soon adopted the same policies: news-gathering, sensationalism, active promotion. Competition increased the tempo. Crimes became more lurid. Scandalous private lives were spread across the pages. The *Herald* became more aggressive in gathering news. It rushed boats to meet incoming ships, to be first with the European news. It established foreign correspondents. After 1844, when the first telegraph line was opened, stories "by telegraph" began to excite readers. A few years later the railroads began carrying papers to out-of-town subscribers. Circulations grew. In all the big cities, newspapers became large and powerful.

Not everyone was happy about the papers. The reporting of crime and scandal was continually protested. People said the papers were corrupting the young and encouraging crime.

A father, protesting to a Boston newspaper, said he would rather see his children "in their graves while pure in innocence, than dwelling with pleasure upon these reports, which have grown so bold."

In 1841, Horace Greeley, launching the *Tribune,* condemned the penny papers for being willing, for private gain, to "fan into destroying flames the hellish passions which now slumber in the bosom of society." He concluded: "The guilt of murder may not stain their hands; but the fouler and more damning guilt of *making murderers.*"

But the penny papers were not inclined to be penitent. To expose crime, they said, was to discourage it. Wherever villainous men deserved exposure, Day had said, he would "lash the rascals naked through the world."

James Gordon Bennett, soon after launching the *Herald,* said with characteristic immodesty: "Books have had their day—the theaters have had their day—the temple of religion has had its day. A newspaper can be made to take the lead of all these in the great movements of human thought and of human civilization. A newspaper can send more souls to Heaven, and save more from Hell, than all the churches and chapels in New York—besides making money at the same time." Within a few years the *Herald* became the biggest money-making paper.

The *Tribune* pursued a more dignified course. *The New York Times,* launched in 1851, was even more restrained. And these papers proved something that must have surprised many people. Somehow, in a few turbulent decades, a new class of readers had grown up: people who wanted news even without emphasis on crime and sex. In 1861, when the sensational *Herald* had a daily circulation of seventy-five thousand, the *Tribune* had fifty-five thousand.

Other papers, as well as magazines and books, seemed to prove the same point. Literary magazines began to flourish. But the sensational press also grew rapidly. In this it received aid from a factor of growing importance: advertising.

THE ADVERTISER. When the penny papers began, they represented a risk. A paper could not be printed for this price. Advertising would have to be the main support of any one-cent paper. Would the risk prove justified?

As circulation bounded, the doubts disappeared. New advertisers flocked to the papers. Now papers could expand, employ more reporters, add more pages, attract more readers —and therefore still more advertisers.

Advertisers were beginning to include not only local stores and services but also factory-made products. Canals and railroads were carrying such products to more and more distant markets. They had to be sold through more and more papers. Thus mass production, and the wide distribution that followed, brought a boom to advertising and to the press.

For a time the advertising field was chaotic. How could a manufacturer in Philadelphia place advertisements in papers in Boston, New York, Baltimore, Washington, Charleston? There were no printed lists of papers, space rates and circulations.

In the midst of this confusion the *advertising agent* entered the picture.

ADVERTISING AGENT. At first, in the 1840's, he was just a man with mysterious lists of papers and secret information about them. He was ready to serve the advertiser as bargainer and space buyer. He was not well thought of but he seemed to be necessary. He generally collected his commission from the papers. That is, he sold space at one rate to the advertiser, bought it at a lower rate from the newspaper. His commissions mounted so rapidly that in the 1850's the *agent* was growing into the *agency*. It began to resemble the modern agency with its assembly line of writers and other experts. The advertising agency was still mainly a space-brokerage firm but began to provide additional services—writing copy and advising on strategy. Its specialty: reaching and influencing people.

For a long time patent medicine provided the chief revenue for advertising agencies, but gradually other clients became important.

During the Civil War advertising got its biggest help from an unexpected source. The United States Treasury decided to push the sale of war bonds by buying advertising space in every Northern newspaper it could find. It handed the job to a New York advertising agency, Peaslee and Company.* Although this gave advertising men a new air of respectability, there were still constant complaints about their business.

But advertising and the press kept growing together.

The Civil War, speeding the growth of railroads, telegraph lines, and factory methods of production, set the stage for a dizzying half century of expansion. It included depressions and panics but the expansion continued. It meant new advertisers and readers for the press. As in Benjamin Day's time, new groups kept entering the reading public.

Immigrants, coming to America by the hundreds of thou-

* Presbrey, Frank Spencer. *The History and Development of Advertising.*

sands annually during the 1860's, 1870's, 1880's, included new readers for the press.

Women, lured from home labors by manufactured goods in stores, were becoming a factor in the national economy. They were becoming buyers and readers. Advertisements and features were being addressed to them. As they entered business, drawn by the typewriter and the jobs it created, newspapers gave still more attention to women. Columns of advice to the lovelorn became common. Numerous magazines for women were being launched.

Farmers, more and more affected by industrial booms and depressions, were becoming increasingly conscious of themselves as a group. They saw new legislation often favoring the manufacturer at the expense of the farmer. They began to organize. Special publications for the farmer grew rapidly.

Workers, including farm boys drawn by the thousands to factories and mines, were becoming readers. In magazines and books they could find an endless supply of stories about boys who rose from rags to riches. Meanwhile worker organizations were developing a growing labor press.

The growth of the reading public was being stimulated by the growth of public schools and, throughout the latter half of the nineteenth century, by the rise of the free library. Illiteracy was in disfavor. Everyone yearned to read.

Against this background it is easy to understand the sensationally successful debut in 1893 of the colored comic strip. For the new and struggling reader—immigrant, woman, farmer, worker—it meant easy, painless reading or semireading.

The first colored strip, "Hogan's Alley," started by the New York Sunday *World* under Joseph Pulitzer, was so successful that it stirred a comic-strip war between Pulitzer's

World and Hearst's *Journal*. The *World* launched a four-page comic supplement; the *Journal* followed with an eight-page comic supplement. They attracted new readers by the hundreds of thousands. Entertainment acquired an increasing role in newspapers.

If the closing decades of the nineteenth century were a period of boom, they were also a period of growing bitterness. They brought huge fortunes but also a growth of slums, squalor, smoke, child labor, tuberculosis, drunkenness, crime, political corruption. The development of mass production was being paralleled by the development of the Salvation Army and the Anti-Saloon League.

The growth of labor unions, forcibly resisted, brought outbursts of terrible violence.

It is not surprising that the journalistic tradition of lashing "the rascals naked through the world" continued with rising intensity through these years of turmoil. For everyone's troubles, the papers provided satisfying scapegoats: trusts, politicians, unions, anarchists, saloonkeepers, foreigners.

The *Journal*, under William Randolph Hearst, was not content with exposure. The *Journal* adopted the slogan: "While others talk, the *Journal* acts." The *Journal* claimed credit for solving a murder. It brought suit in the courts to correct evil conditions. In 1898, when the battleship *Maine* exploded in the harbor of Havana, it offered fifty thousand dollars reward for information. Headlines screamed: "THE WARSHIP *Maine* WAS SPLIT IN TWO BY AN ENEMY'S SECRET INFERNAL MACHINE." It developed feeling to such fever pitch that when war began, the *Journal* was felt to have forced the nation's hand and made war inevitable. The *Journal's* circulation passed one million.

A hundred years earlier, at the beginning of the nineteenth century, papers had waited for news to come to them. By mid-century they were sending reporters everywhere in search of news. By the end of the century they were making news.

Making news now began to grow into a major occupation. But a new figure was to take it over.

The growing power of the press was giving impetus to a novel type of middleman. The *press agent* had for some time existed in the circus field, but not in business. Now corporations, alarmed by the growing protests against "trusts," were beginning to hire writers to send to the press news stories about corporation accomplishments. The purpose, as the company saw it, was to make sure that the company's side of the story was adequately reported.

Just as the advertising agency concerned itself with obtaining and using bought advertising space, the press agent began to concern himself with obtaining and using free space through news stories, articles, entertainment features. The press agent was welcomed and resented by the press. He was welcomed as an unpaid reporter and resented as a nonpaying advertiser. He was resented as a contriver of events and welcomed for the excitement he brought. The press agent gradually became a fixture in business, government, political parties, labor unions and every sort of citizen group. Every kind of organization began to concern itself with the contents of the press.

Meanwhile the press, pushed by the industrial spiral, grew and grew. As it grew it became somewhat more conservative. The era of "personal journalism" began to decline. A more gigantic, more impersonal journalism took its place.

New inventions and ideas kept helping the giant grow. Since the 1880's it had become possible, through the halftone, to reproduce photographs. Press associations were making it possible for newspapers to obtain national and international news at low cost. Feature syndicates brought them, also at low cost, special columns, cartoons, and serialized novels by famous writers.

The development of newspaper chains was cutting costs, and applying to newspaper publishing the economies of big-business methods.

The women's publications were having a miraculous growth. Women were the new spenders. They were becoming the darlings of the American economy. In 1900, the *Ladies' Home Journal* acquired a paid circulation of a million copies, at ten cents a copy.

Specialized publications of all kinds were springing up. All sorts of economic groups were forming associations, resisting attacks, exchanging ideas. There were trade papers for every conceivable kind of group.

Newspapers, magazines, books, all were booming. It seemed as if America would be engulfed in a tidal wave of paper.

But now, for a moment, we must go back and pick up another thread.

2 The Moving Image

In the days when Johann Gutenberg's Bible, printed from movable type, was stirring wonder in Germany, another innovation was gaining a foothold in Italy. It was a kind of game, having at first no apparent relationship to the dissemination of information or ideas.

The device was described in Leonardo da Vinci's unpublished notes. If on a sunny day you sit in a darkened room with only a pinhole open on one side, you see on an opposite wall or other surface images of the outside world—a tree, a man, a passing carriage.

The principle was described in detail in the book, *Natural Magic,* by Giovanni Battista della Porta, published in 1558. A few years later it became known that a lens, in place of the pinhole, would sharpen the image.

A group of people in a darkened room, watching images on a wall—thrown by a beam of light cutting through the darkness—must have resembled a group watching home movies. There was one difference: the picture was upside down.

Presently the lens was being put in one side of a box instead of in the wall of a room. Through mirrors, the image could be thrown on a glass screen in the box, and seen right side up.

The box, still thought of as a small room, was called a "dark room" or *"camera obscura."* This camera could be aimed at a landscape, street, garden party. A group of people looking in amazement at the moving images in the box may well have resembled a group watching television.

Magicians began using the device for mystification and delight. It became a pastime among the well-to-do throughout Europe.

By the 1600's, painters in many countries were using it to solve problems of perspective. Some artists found it easier to trace the two-dimensional image of the *camera obscura* than to work from three-dimensional reality.

The next step was obvious. Could the image be preserved, saving the artist even more work? The idea seems to have been present for two centuries, awaiting the development of chemistry—and of demand.

The demand came early in the nineteenth century. The same social pressure that brought the *Sun's* circulation in two years to twenty thousand copies, that made Benjamin Day and other publishers turn to new presses, new paper and steam power to fill the demand, this same pressure operated now toward the development of the camera.

With the breakdown of old class barriers in Europe and America, the new groups rising in affluence wanted portrait paintings. For centuries the portrait on the wall had been a mark of social standing. Institutional advertising, we might call it today. It was natural that the newly prosperous merchant, or the mechanic grown into a manufacturer, should want this badge of status. During the early years of the nineteenth century the demand for portrait paintings was growing as never before.

What was more natural than that artists should be thinking increasingly about the *camera obscura?* And that one artist, Louis Daguerre, should turn to the chemist, Joseph Nicéphore Niepce, and propose a working alliance? The aim —to preserve the *camera* image.

The artist and the chemist began their collaboration in 1829. A few years later Niepce died, but Daguerre, nearing a solution, carried on. In 1839 he announced that he had solved the problem. There was excitement throughout Europe.

Within a year the American artist, Samuel F. B. Morse, who like Daguerre had scientific leanings, was taking pictures of his wife and daughter on a Manhattan rooftop. By 1850 there were seventy-one daguerreotype galleries in New York.

In the 1860's, in the Civil War, the camera was functioning as reporter.

The 1870's saw the beginning of a curious experiment. Governor Leland Stanford of California made a bet. He had maintained that a galloping horse's four hoofs are, at one moment, simultaneously off the ground. To settle the matter he engaged Eadweard Muybridge, a photographer. Muybridge placed a long series of cameras in a row, in such a way that pictures would be shot in rapid succession as a horse galloped past. The pictures proved Stanford's point.

Later Muybridge fastened a series of such pictures on the edge of a disc. Only one picture could be seen at one time, through an aperture in front of the disc. When the disc was rotated rapidly, the illusion of a running horse was produced.

About 1880 he projected such pictures on a screen and called the projector a "zoopraxiscope." What the zoopraxiscope projected was a motion picture, but the system was not very efficient. Dozens of cameras were needed to produce an effect lasting only a few seconds. Yet Muybridge had provided incentive for more skillful technicians.

In 1889, Thomas Edison read about a new product developed by George Eastman of Rochester. It was a boon for the amateur photographer. Eastman was marketing a continuous roll of transparent film, to do away with the nuisance of a separate plate for each picture. Thomas Edison sent for a roll of the film.

To Edison it did not seem inconceivable that such a strip of film should move rapidly, in a series of jerks, within a camera that would take a dozen or more pictures each second. Within months he demonstrated the idea, showing the pictures in an instrument he called a "kinetoscope."

By 1894 operators of penny arcades were buying and featuring kinetoscopes. By depositing a penny in a kinetoscope you could see a minute or more of a wiggling dancer or a sparring boxer. You peered into the kinetoscope, as people had peered long before into a *camera obscura*.

But the economics of the device were not promising. If the picture could be thrown on a screen, many would be able to see it simultaneously.

Both in America and in Europe, this problem was soon

solved. In France, Auguste and Louis Lumière unveiled their *Cinématographe*. In America parallel experimentation produced the Edison vitascope.

In 1896, at Koster and Bial's Music Hall in New York City, an amazed audience saw on a screen a comedy boxing match, a "skirt dance," an "umbrella dance," a "butterfly dance," a military parade. The excitement spread rapidly.

At the penny arcades the operators were soon closing off tiny rooms to accommodate small audiences. An eager stream of visitors came to look.

Vaudeville men also gave the novelty some attention but the penny arcade people were more eager. Some arcade operators were so impressed with the new attraction that they searched for larger quarters. Soon stores were being converted for moving-picture showings. One operator, charging five cents, called his show place a "nickelodeon." The name struck the popular fancy. By 1907 in all the larger American cities nickelodeons were spreading, according to *Harper's Weekly,* "as thickly as saloons." They offered an hour's show of many short items.

A few saloons, fearful of the competition, installed screens and projectors. But they could not stop the flood of people who moved hour by hour in and out of the dark nickelodeons. Who were these thousands and hundreds of thousands?

They were not being drawn from the live theater. Much of the nickelodeon audience had never been in a theater. Like the audience that launched the penny papers, it was a new audience.

During these years the streams of immigration to the United States were turning into a tidal wave. In 1905, 1,026,499 immigrants arrived. In 1906 there were 1,100,735 immigrants. In 1907, 1,285,349 immigrants. Most poured into the already crowded slums of the big cities. On arriving many could not speak English. Many could not read. But the moving picture in the nickelodeons gave them an immediate relationship to their new world. For ease and vividness of communication, it outdid the comic strip.

It spoke to them in the most direct terms. Often there were stories kidding new immigrants. There were policemen, funny and serious, and the troubles they had with burglars and tramps. There were farces about erring husbands and wives. There were fake trips to the moon.

Comedy, romance, crime, conflict, adventure. The larger cities acquired hundreds of nickelodeons.

But not everyone was happy about them. Their obsession with scandal and crime brought angry denunciations. In 1907 the Chicago *Tribune* charged that nickelodeons were "ministering to the lowest passions of children." A letter from a judge was printed: "Those nickelodeons indirectly or directly caused more juvenile crimes coming into this court than all other causes combined." *Good Housekeeping* condemned the nickelodeons as "a primary school for criminals."

While some saw the moving picture as causing moral havoc, others began to see its power as a solution to countless problems. Various magazine articles of 1909 to 1914 depicted the new medium as a kind of cure-all. Some of the titles of the period were:

Curing Truants by the Movies

Edison Versus Euclid: Has He Invented a Moving Stairway to Learning?

Making Americans by Motion Pictures

Motion Pictures To Make Good Citizens

Motion Pictures To Prevent Wrecks

Movies in Church and out
Fighting Disease with the Motion Picture
Movies Speed Up Labor

Meanwhile, in another part of the world, Lenin was say-ing: "When the masses take possession of the film and it comes into the hands of true supporters of socialist culture, it will become one of the most powerful means of educating the masses." *

But the men who made the motion pictures had little reason to be interested in propaganda, uplift or education. Nickels were coming in at a fantastic rate, and the nature of the drawing power seemed clear.

In 1908, the film *After Many Years,* directed by D. W. Griffith and based on Tennyson's *Enoch Arden,* featured a historic innovation. Until then all scenes had been shot at a fixed distance, usually in long shot or medium shot. The audience saw the actors in somewhat the same perspective as figures on the stage.

Now suddenly, in the middle of a scene, came a giant close-up. It had an astonishing impact.

The close-up began to give audiences a new kind of intimacy with the heroes and heroines of story. Soon films were full of close-ups. Soon millions of men knew, more exactly than the features of their own wives, the tilt of a movie heroine's nose and the arch of her eyebrow. It is no accident that the star system began a year or two after Griffith's use of close-up.

For years the nickelodeon operators had advertised films by their titles only. Presently the formula became:

* Inkeles, Alex., *Public Opinion in Soviet Russia: A Study in Mass Per-suasion.* Cambridge: Harvard University Press. 1950.

Mary Pickford

in

Poor Little Rich Girl

By 1914, Mary Pickford was being signed to a contract for $104,000 a year.

By that time the feature-length picture was established and began to dominate the market. It helped build the glamor of the star. The short items dwindled. Among them only newsreels and cartoon films gained in importance. Educational shorts declined.

By that time film men were becoming more respectable in business matters. At first they had freely taken copyrighted literary material. Now chastened by lawsuits—one producer was penalized twenty-five thousand dollars for unauthorized use of *Ben Hur*—they were beginning to pay for story rights. Intercompany patent disputes, once marked by physical violence, were turning to legal procedures.

By that time the film was outgrowing the converted stores, the small flea traps. The movie men were beginning to build huge theater palaces with balconies, carpeted stairways, brass railings and spittoons. Soon they would have ushers in brocaded uniforms.

By that time, too, the film industry was migrating westward and building in Hollywood a new colony far removed from its slum beginnings.

Soon this colony would grow rich and powerful beyond all expectations—for reasons that had little to do with the making of movies.

In 1914, the outbreak of World War I in Europe closed every European motion-picture studio. But the countries of

Europe were, like America, dotted with movie houses ranging from converted stores to theater palaces. The war-locked nations were hungry for film and the American film industry was ready to supply it.

Now the international flavor of its earliest audiences, with their heavy concentration of immigrants, was of special value to the American film industry. What had pleased the immigrants in New York, Chicago and other American cities was equally welcome throughout Europe. The American film built a powerful bridge across the world. Millions everywhere loved Mary Pickford, quivered with excitement and guilt over Theda Bara, laughed and wept for Charlie Chaplin. In 1916, Charlie Chaplin signed a contract for $670,000 per year.

When America's 1917 entry into the war turned the tide of battle, America became irrevocably a major world power. And Hollywood became a world film capital.

America was to learn that world leadership was no comfortable mantle. Hollywood learned the same thing.

All sorts of interests—governmental, financial, political, religious—began to concern themselves with Hollywood's productions. All were anxious to show the film men how to use, or not use, their seeming power over men's minds.

Hollywood became the new arena for the press agent, now growing into a *publicity man* and presently a *public relations representative* or an *information specialist*.

Hollywood, having geared its operations to a huge market, had become dependent on it. Fearful of alienating any large segment of it, film makers became more and more averse to controversy.

They erected for themselves an ideal called Entertainment —visualized as something remote from current problems.

Actually the ideal was always unattainable. A story that seems to one person the purest diversion, even a flight from reality, seems to another full of propaganda implications. But the Hollywood film industry, with its world-wide commitments, could not help pursuing the elusive ideal.*

In the hope of warding off trouble, the major motion-picture companies in 1922 engaged Will H. Hays, Postmaster General under President Harding, to be czar of the film industry. Under him it later developed a strict system of self-censorship.

All this did not succeed in abolishing outside interference. A few states had set up censor boards to pass on the fitness of films to be shown in public. These continued their work. Some cities also maintained censors. Religious and other groups maintained committees to review films and publish ratings of approval or disapproval.

To many it seemed that Hollywood, hemmed in by pressures, was pushed more and more toward pictures regarded as "safe." There were magnificent, powerful exceptions. But to educators Hollywood seemed more and more a dream factory. It seemed to them that if film was to turn educator, it must be through channels other than Hollywood and the theaters it served.

This led in 1923 to an important decision.

Until then few schools, churches and other local oganizations had bought projectors. They were discouraged by many factors. The film used in theaters was inflammable and required a fireproof projection booth. Projectors were huge

* On an ironic occasion in 1956, President Sukarno of Indonesia visited Hollywood and, to its surprise, thanked the film industry for its aid to the national revolutions of postwar Asia. By showing ordinary people with refrigerators and cars, he said, American films had "helped to build up a sense of deprivation of man's birthright." He told the assembled executives: "That is why I say you are revolutionaries, and that is why I salute you. In a world of inequality, you and your products cannot be noncontroversial."

and expensive. Film reels, in the 35 mm width used in theaters, were bulky and expensive.

A few companies had tried to introduce more convenient, inexpensive systems: smaller projectors, and a narrow width of film to go with them. Equipment and films had been offered in widths of 28 mm, 22 mm, 21 mm, 17½ mm, 16 mm, 15 mm, 11 mm, 9.5 mm.* The confusion of widths paralyzed the market. Schools were unlikely to buy a projector that could show films of only one company.

Then came agreement. In 1923 the Eastman Kodak Company, the Victor Animatograph Corporation, Bell and Howell and others resolved on a standard width for nontheater films and projectors: 16 mm. They also agreed on a noninflammable film.

These decisions laid the basis for a new exhibition network in school, church, club, office, hospital, camp and home. The prospect of a new kind of market began to stimulate new kinds of production—slowly at first.

Already there had been experimentation toward the kinds of films needed.

As early as 1908 the U. S. Department of Agriculture had entered film production.

In 1911, the U. S. Department of the Interior had produced a film to urge farm migration to newly opened Western lands.

In 1916, the Ford Motor Company had begun to make educational films.

During World War I the Army had used training films.

In 1918, the Girl Scouts of the U. S. A. had made a film on its activtities.

In 1922, Robert Flaherty's *Nanook of the North,* spon-

---

* *Sixty Years of 16 mm Film: 1923–1983.* A Symposium. Evanston: Film Council of America, 1954.

sored by Revillon Frères as a public relations project, had made its appearance.

Such films, previously made for theater use, pointed the way for the 16 mm film field. But for the moment the 16 mm film was small business.

Hollywood was booming and still growing. Its men and women were gods and goddesses who set styles in clothes, hairdos, morals, daydreams, literature.

The fear that movies would wipe out reading had proved ill founded. A new fan-magazine industry was built on movie worship. Newspapers, at first hostile to films, began to feature film news to attract new readers. Film advertising brought new revenue to newspapers and magazines. When Hollywood adapted classics, libraries had runs on them. "Motion-picture editions" were published. Rudolph Valentino, Lon Chaney and Douglas Fairbanks were creating readers.

The educator might be critical but the public was not. The theater palace was the new temple of civilization.

The year 1926 brought an agony of readjustment: the coming of the sound film. Then 1929 brought another: the stock-market crash. The film industry survived these, going on to new triumphs. With the coming of World War II, film proved itself as trainer, educator, propagandist. The 16 mm film boomed. Another development, the film strip, boomed with it. Meanwhile the rise of microfilm was making film, like paper, important as a storehouse of knowledge. Now film laboratories were feeding not only theaters and drive-ins but also schools, colleges, camps, churches, clubs, offices, libraries, hospitals, Grange halls, homes. It seemed as if America would be engulfed in a flood of film.

But now once more we must go back and pick up another thread.

3 Signals in the Air

In 1558, Giovanni Battista della Porta, whose book on *Natural Magic* explained the *camera obscura,* also described a *sympathetic telegraph.* This was a proposed message-sending device that was to utilize magnetism—a phenomenon known since ancient times.

A number of other thinkers amused themselves with this idea. But for the moment it remained speculation, awaiting further knowledge of physics and the pressure of need.

Both the knowledge and the need arrived in the nineteenth century.

The development of the electromagnet early in the century made the telegraph possible. The growth of mass production and distribution made it necessary. Never had there been such pressure for quick and efficient message services to distant points.

Wherever industrialization was going on, men were becoming dependent on events in distant places: distant sources of supply and distant markets. This kind of enterprise demanded more than courier and carrier-pigeon communication. Rapid intelligence became a life and death matter.

Thus the stage was set for Samuel F. B. Morse, one of the patriarchs of communication. In 1840, he had become one of America's first daguerreotypists. Now, in 1844, he clicked out, from Washington to Baltimore, the first message by electromagnetic telegraph: "What hath God wrought?" The carrier pigeon's days were numbered.

Soon overhead wires were connecting all the principal cities. Ocean-bottom cables were planned and laid. But the pressure continued. Throughout the Civil War, railroad tracks and overhead wires pushed farther and farther. By 1876, Alexander Graham Bell was showing that overhead wires and cables could carry not only dots and dashes but also human speech.

Now telegraph and telephone, both aiding the rapid geographic expansion of business, helped build up pressure for still more message services.

These pressures led in several directions. In 1877, Thomas Edison was fastening a needle to a telephone mouthpiece and studying its vibrations. He tried to find ways of preserving the pattern of those vibrations—first on paraffin paper, then on tinfoil, later on wax—so that the sounds could be repeated. He saw his invention as an aid to efficient communication in business, and perhaps in education.

In 1896, Guglielmo Marconi, Irish-Italian youth of twenty-two, revealed that dots and dashes could hurtle space without wires or cables. It was only a matter of time before speech would do the same. Fessenden and de Forest showed that it could be done.

Soon many countries began to experiment with wireless—or "radio." By World War I scores of radio transmitters were active in the United States. They had, for the moment, nothing to do with entertainment. For shipping companies radio meant greater safety and a means of directing banana boats to profitable markets. For the armed forces radio meant priceless intelligence and co-ordination, in offense and defense.

World War I dramatized the value of radio and aroused public excitement, especially among the young. A great postwar future was foreseen for radio—a future of rescues at sea, espionage and counterespionage, detection of smugglers, direction of planes to lost explorers, exchange of mes-

THE DAILY GRAPHIC

An Illustrated Evening Newspaper

39 & 41 PARK PLACE.

| VOL. XIII. | All the News. Four Editions Daily. | NEW YORK, THURSDAY, MARCH 15, 1877. | $15 Per Year in Advance. Single Copies, Five Cents. | NO. 1246. |

TERRORS OF THE TELEPHONE—THE ORATOR OF THE FUTURE.

sages with island outposts. In short, a future of point-to-point communication.

It had, all this time, nothing to do with entertainment, news, or the reaching of millions. Except, perhaps, in the imaginations of a few.

While the pressures of the industrial age were building a varied message service, a few observers had ideas that led in other directions.

Back in 1877, just after the invention of the telephone, a cartoonist had published a drawing titled *Terrors of the Telephone*. It showed an orator at a telephone mouthpiece addressing audiences in Boston, San Francisco, London, Dublin, Peking and the Fiji Islands, as well as an American Indian on the Western plains. The artist's vision of the broadcast age was apparently not taken seriously by his public.

In 1916, a telegrapher working for the American Marconi Company in New York wrote a memorandum to his superiors. This young man, David Sarnoff, had been at his wireless set in 1912 when news arrived of the Titanic's collision with an iceberg. Sarnoff had received and announced the shocking news, and for grueling hours had stayed at his key, to direct rescue ships to the scene. Now, four years later, he had some suggestions on the future of radio:

I have in mind a plan of development which would make radio a household utility. . . . The idea is to bring music into the home by wireless. . . . The receiver can be designed in the form of a simple "Radio Music Box" and arranged for several different wave lengths, which should be changeable with the throwing of a single switch or the pressing of a single button. . . . The same principle can be extended to numerous other fields, as for example receiving lectures at home, which would be perfectly audible; also events of national importance can be simultaneously announced and received. Baseball scores can be transmitted in the air. . . . This proposition would be especially interesting to farmers and others living in outlying districts. . . .

But these ideas seemed remote and visionary in 1916. Even in 1919, when the Radio Corporation of America was formed and took over the assets of American Marconi, the purpose was not "music . . . lectures . . . events . . . baseball scores." The purpose was the message business.

The same purpose guided other corporations interesting themselves in radio: General Electric, American Telephone and Telegraph, Westinghouse.

Radio was thought of, in 1920, as a message service that had enormous value but one fatal weakness: lack of privacy. This flaw seemed troublesome.

All over the United States, boys excited by stories of wartime radio were tinkering with sets. Some were building receivers, carefully winding wires around empty Quaker Oats boxes. They listened to everything. Others wanted to be senders, filling the air with code and talk. What could be done about this lack of privacy?

A Westinghouse researcher named Frank Conrad kept sending radio messages from an experimental transmitter in his garage—Station 8XK, Pittsburgh. The idea was to test and improve equipment. While an assistant checked reception quality elsewhere, Conrad would talk, read aloud from newspapers, or play phonograph records—the same ones over and over.

Presently Conrad began to get post cards from eavesdropping listeners, criticizing his musical tastes and requesting more variety. Sometimes the writers suggested particular numbers. Since the post cards gave Conrad information on the range of his transmitter, he encouraged them by complying with the requests. Thus he became, in the interests of research, an early disc jockey.

Presently a Pittsburgh department store began to advertise radio receivers for "those who want to tune in the Westinghouse station." The Westinghouse organization was astonished. It had stumbled, unknowingly, into a new era.

Westinghouse now glimpsed the future and moved toward it. It announced that it would transmit the presidential election returns on November 2, 1920, via a new and more powerful transmitter—100 watts. Many sets were bought in anticipation. Thus the victory of Warren G. Harding over James M. Cox was "broadcast" in the formal launching of Station KDKA.

The same sort of thing was happening in other parts of the country. Everywhere the eavesdroppers were turning into "ladies and gentlemen of the radio audience." Broadcasting, accidental offspring of the message business, was on its way.

In 1921 the Dempsey-Carpentier fight for the heavyweight championship of the world was broadcast from Boyle's Thirty Acres in New Jersey. Thousands of sets were bought in anticipation. In 1920 and 1921 the public spent millions of dollars on sets. Manufacturers could not meet demand. The high-school set tinkerers, a new audience, had done the missionary work. They were now being joined by a fast-growing host of listeners.

Just as swiftly, new stations sprang up. They did not yet sell time for advertising, but most had a commercial purpose. A radio station was thought of as a novel and inexpensive means of publicity for any sort of company. A hotel or department store or newspaper might put a transmitter on its roof and outfit a small room or closet with amplifying and control equipment, microphone and phonograph. Total investment, in the early 1920's, might not exceed two thousand dollars.

Personnel needs worried no one. All you had to have was an engineer. He would play records and sometimes read newspaper items. Volunteers would perhaps drop in and read a poem or tell a story. It was as informal as an early newspaper.

It seemed to occur to no one that broadcast use of copyright material might involve legal problems. As with early newspapers and films, everything was freely taken.

Now and then the station would mention its call letters and the company or organization it represented.

Radio listening had a restless pattern. Stations assumed, correctly, that most listeners were constantly scouring the dial, trying to get Denver, Cincinnati, Detroit, Cleveland, Pittsburgh, Minneapolis. There was therefore no reason for a station to think about "programming." The broadcaster merely hoped that each night some thousands of people, exploring the fascinating wasteland of outer space, would suddenly, for a moment, come on *his* hotel, *his* store, *his* newspaper. And there, amid static, squeals and maddening fadeouts, a mysterious bond of friendship would be established.

Someday, perhaps months later, a traveler on his summer vacation would stop his roadster in front of the hotel, the store, the newspaper office and come in beaming all over, saying, "We got you several times last winter. I wanted to drop in and say hello."

For just this kind of good will, radio stations were started in the early 1920's by automobile dealers, appliance stores, radio repair shops, publishers, utilities, manufacturers, banks, clothing stores, furniture stores, restaurants, theaters, creameries.

Stations were also started by religious organizations. This was logical enough. Had not Jesus said, "What you hear in the ear, proclaim upon the housetops"?

Dozens of stations were started by educational organizations. This too was logical. What would a teacher not give for the kind of dedication he had seen in the radio-crazy youngsters? Here was a force to be harnessed for education. But before long, it was hoped, these young listeners would be hearing not merely trivialities but worth-while educational material.

For the school-owned and college-owned stations, disillusionment began quickly. For a while it was easy to persuade professors to visit the cramped, monk's-cloth-draped studio and, without extra remuneration, speak a lecture. For a while the pioneering feeling was powerful. But it all took time. Enthusiasm lagged.

Some college stations tried putting microphones into regular classrooms but the acoustics were generally disastrous. Many educational broadcasters gave up early.

Meanwhile the commercially owned stations had their troubles too. In 1922, the American Society of Composers, Authors and Publishers issued an ultimatum. Henceforth commercial stations would pay royalties for the use of copyrighted music. ASCAP proposed annual license fees for stations.

The broadcasters were outraged but ASCAP won its point.

It is no accident that in that same year, 1922, station WEAF in New York inaugurated a new practice: the selling of time. It sold time for the promotion of real-estate lots in Long Island.

The practice spread quickly. Magazine articles and speeches protested against it, but they had little effect. Secretary of Commerce Herbert Hoover said it was "unthinkable" that this great educational instrument should be used for "direct" advertising. But even as he spoke, broadcasters were selling periods of time for toothpastes, cigars, cigarettes, candy bars, chewing gum.

The establishment in 1926 of the Federal Radio Commission * for traffic supervision of the air waves in no way halted the trend to advertising.

At first radio advertising tended to be polite and formal. But this did not last long. Some announcers developed a thundering style of salesmanship. Some discovered intimacy and whispered their messages, becoming soul mates to millions. Commercial jingles made their appearance. Merchandising schemes began: a listener, by sending in a Forhan's box top with the hour and date of his birth, could have his fortune told over the air by an astrologer.

The power of personality began to be appreciated and live talent of various kinds flocked to the stations: announcers, crooners, monologists. With advertising revenue, there was money to pay them—small money, at first.

Radio listening was changing its pattern. Listeners no longer roamed. They began to develop loyalties. Here and there, obscure announcers and crooners became public idols. The idolatry had commercial value. More advertisers became interested.

At first radio was a nuisance to advertising agencies because they had to deal with each station separately. But the National Broadcasting Company was formed in 1926 and the Columbia Broadcasting System in 1927. Now one transaction could buy a whole group of stations, linked by wire.

* Superseded in 1934 by the Federal Communications Commission.

The pattern of radio was taking shape. Then came the 1929 stock-market crash.

In the depression years that followed, vaudeville almost disappeared. In countless cities, long-established theatrical stock companies vanished. Night clubs closed. Concert audiences dwindled. What happened to radio?

It became apparent that the people staying away from theater, club and concert were listening to their radios.

Social workers reported cases of families that had lost their installment-bought car, icebox, vacuum cleaner and sofa and canceled the milk but still met payments on the radio. It was their link with humanity.

Radio philosophers like Kate Smith and Tony Wons became national figures and got thousands of letters each week asking advice on personal problems.

If advertisers needed more evidence of the emotional grip of radio they found it in politics. Franklin D. Roosevelt, opposed by an overwhelming majority of the nation's newspapers, won decisively over Herbert Hoover. Roosevelt's election and later re-elections were ascribed in part to his mastery of radio technique.

The rise of Hitler in Germany further dramatized the power of radio.

A number of advertisers, hit hard by depression, began to make a comeback with the help of radio.

All this brought in more sponsors. In their wake came comedians from vaudeville, actors and dramatists from the theater, musicians from night club and concert. Radio was booming. Sets in use in the United States rose:

1930	14,750,000
1935	26,006,000
1940	45,000,000

Radio advertising expenditures rose:

1930	$ 60,000,000
1935	$105,000,000
1940	$200,000,000

But not everyone admired radio. As the air became filled with crooners and singing commercials, then with daytime serials and violent children's programs, then with murder and horror mystery, then with quizzes and giveaways, radio became a favorite target for scorn and indignation.

The criticism rose as a mounting obbligato to the growth of radio. Climaxing the criticism was a cry of dismay from Lee de Forest, asking a convention of broadcasters what they had done to his child. "You have made of him," he said, "a laughingstock to intelligence, surely a stench in the nostrils of the gods of the ionosphere. . . . Murder mysteries rule the waves by night and children are rendered psychopathic by your bedtime stories. This child of mine . . . is maintained moronic, as though you and your sponsors believe the majority of listeners have only moron minds."

Such criticism did not seem to affect listening habits. But it made broadcasters uneasy. During the 1930's the major networks adopted stricter program policies, published codes, and spent increasing amounts on public-service programs. Usually unsponsored, these included symphony orchestras, classic plays, documentaries, forums, news and special-event broadcasts.

During the early 1930's a bitter feud between radio and the newspaper publishers kept down the amount of news on the air. But during the late 1930's the press associations began to serve radio as well as newspapers. Radio meanwhile built its own news-gathering organizations, developed its own correspondents. Broadcasts from Europe became regular.

As Hitler began to threaten the peace of Europe, radio's news programs gripped more and more listeners. A jittery nation awaited war to the accompaniment of almost continual commentary by H. V. Kaltenborn and other analysts. When war started, listening increased still further.

Meanwhile radio, having dug deep roots during depression and grown strong with the coming of war, received new nourishment from an unexpected source: the excess-profits tax.

With the start of war production, a Federal tax of 90 per cent was levied on corporation profits in the highest brackets. Many of the largest companies were producing war materials and had little to sell to the public. But they were anxious to keep their names before the public to meet postwar competition. The soundness of this policy had been established during the period of World War I.

As a result, funds that would otherwise have gone almost wholly into taxes were now spent on *institutional advertising*. Much of this went into radio.

Cultural programs that had seldom been able to attract sponsorship now acquired sponsors, seeking prestige rather than sales. The NBC Symphony Orchestra and the New York Philharmonic had sponsors.

At the same time, intellectuals had been discovering radio. Verse plays were being written by Archibald MacLeish, Stephen Vincent Benét, Edna St. Vincent Millay. As World War II ended, radio stood high in prestige and power.

Then came television.

Throughout the rise of radio, television had been in the background, first as an idea, then as a laboratory item. In the late 1920's there were occasional program experiments. Beginning in 1936 there were frequent telecasts, still on an experimental basis. In special network studios the experimenters suffered in intense heat. Because of unsolved technical problems, actors wore gruesome purple lipstick.

In 1939 a regular schedule of telecasting began. But soon war halted it. Manufacturing facilities were being converted for war-needed electronic equipment.

In several cities television sets were installed in police stations and air-raid wardens watched telecast demonstrations. But on the whole, television lived in suspended animation.

After the war, factories geared for enormous output of electronic equipment suddenly ceased war production, and became available for peacetime uses. Now there was every incentive to push television.

In the intervening years technical progress had been made. In 1945, RCA launched its sensitive Image Orthicon tube, reducing the need for intense light and ghoulish make-up. Low temperature lighting was now also available.

Engineers, performers and sponsors were ready for television. The taverns, pioneer promoters for each medium, were ready. So was the public.

Now a period of explosive growth, comparable to those which had launched the modern newspaper, motion picture and radio, catapulted television into the spotlight. Almost overnight it became the medium that sponsors turned to for prestige. It became the medium that created astonishing sales increases overnight. Obscure politicians, conducting televised hearings, became presidential timber.

All over the nation the television antennas went up—on shack, farm, tenement, apartment house, suburban home.

Living rooms were redesigned. Television chairs, television snack tables, and quick-frozen television suppers appeared on the market.

But, of course, not everyone was happy. Some educators, seeking to establish nonprofit educational stations, were severely critical of boomtime television. A committee of researchers reported that in one broadcast week in January, 1953, New York television viewers could witness 3,421 "acts or threats" of violence. The average rate was said to be 15.2 acts or threats an hour during periods when children were most likely to be watching.

"The terror comic strips were bad enough," wrote Norman Cousins in the *Saturday Review,* "but they are rapidly on their way to playing a squeaky second fiddle to television as prime movers in juvenile misconduct and delinquency."

But the boom continued. Television became the bull's-eye for press agents, publicity men, public-relations consultants, information specialists, public-education directors, and departments of public information.

The fear that broadcasting would reduce literacy had long proved groundless. Broadcast interviews and adaptations stimulated book sales and library use. Broadcast news seemed at first to compete with newspapers but in the long run to stimulate news reading. Magazines of news review and interpretation such as *Time, Newsweek, U. S. News and World Report, The Reporter* and others grew as radio and television grew. Television at first hurt Hollywood, then helped it toward a new boom. Sales of recordings also rose to new levels.

As the second half of the twentieth century began, every medium seemed to be stimulating every other medium. In the United States 60,000,000 people were going to the movies each week. Americans were buying books at the rate of 500,000,000 per year. About 3,500,000,000 copies of periodicals were being distributed. Every man, woman and child in the United States was consuming annually "better than 300 pounds of paper." * And the average viewer watched television three hours per day.

4 Of Words and Mousetraps

Now, with the communications revolution approaching a climax, one asks, "What are its results?" As with many revolutions, they are not quite what might be expected. They are not exactly what prophets predicted. In some respects, they are the opposite.

To get a clear perspective, let us look back once more.

One of the first daily newspapers in the United States was the New York *Daily Advertiser*. Launched in 1785, it was hand-set, hand-printed. It charged three shillings for an advertisement.

Looking back at its advertising, we may find it naïve, primitive, ineffectual. On January 16, 1789, its advertisements included the following:

American Woolens.

JUST received from the flourishing Manufactory at *Hartford*, a few Pieces of superfine BROAD-CLOTHS, *of an excellent quality*, which may be had in patterns, at reasonable prices, of GILBERT EVERINGHAM, No. 44, Water-street,—both London Smoke, and Hartford Grey.

Shopkeepers and others, who may want by the piece or package, will please to leave orders with NATHANIEL HAZARD, No. 51, *Water-street*.

Jan. 13.   m tb tf

* Burlingame, Roger. "Mountains of Paper." In *Harper's* Magazine, October, 1950.

This advertisement may to a modern advertiser seem to have little to recommend it. It does little to attract attention, engage emotion, or any of the things we know to be essential.

But in looking at it casually, one may miss its secret—a very potent ingredient. It is simply this: cloth was scarce.

Clothing material and clothing were not yet in mass production. Throughout recorded history demand for these, as for almost everything else, exceeded supply. People needed clothing. They needed it so badly that *the buyer sought the product—not the product the buyer.*

All this would have made it absurd for Gilbert Everingham to shout his message. The fact that he had the stuff was drama itself.

After reading this advertisement George Washington, newly elected President of the United States, wrote to a Major General in New York, asking him to buy some of the material immediately, "enough to make me a suit of cloaths. As to the colour, I shall leave it altogether to your taste." This advertisement had impact.

Today clothing needs are supplied largely by ready-made clothes, promoted through press, film, radio, television at a cost of hundreds of millions of dollars per year.

The cloth merchant of 1789 could easily tell what results he got from his three-shilling advertisement.

Today a clothing manufacturer, spending twenty-thousand dollars for one full-color advertisement in a mass-circulation magazine, is not sure what results he gets. But he feels certain that unless he continues such advertising, as well as supporting promotion in the trade press, his salesmen will have a harder time selling his products to the dealers who must sell them to the public.

Sometimes the manufacturer is baffled as to why one line of clothing is a success while another goes unsold. Is the product wrong? Is his advertising wrong? Is it reaching the wrong audience? Does it have, for some people, unguessed implications of a wrong sort?

The answers to such questions may be worth millions. So he goes in for audience research, market research. He turns to the sociologist and gets detailed reports on this and that population segment: what it is doing, buying, joining, reading, hearing, watching, saying. He can use all this. But he also needs to know reasons. So he turns for additional help to the psychologist, for *motivation research* on the consumer.

The psychologist is ready to serve—with *depth interviews, thematic apperception tests,* and other devices. But he warns that the answers are not simple, not pat. The *whys* of any act or failure to act, the psychologist says, include:

> The *whys* a person can talk about directly, freely and factually.
>
> The *whys* a person talks about but which are distortions of fact.
>
> The *whys* a person doesn't want to talk about because he feels touchy about them.
>
> The *whys* a person can't talk about because he doesn't know they exist.*

Thus the modern manufacturer, reaching out to a public he cannot see, finds his communication problems growing with his business.

Mass media, important in the distribution of goods, are also important in the circulation of ideas. So it was with the New York *Daily Advertiser*.

* *Motivation Research.* A promotion brochure of Dunlap and Associates, Inc., Stamford, Conn.

Two years before the election of George Washington, our country faced a crisis. The governmental machinery was not functioning. A proposed new constitution, providing for a stronger central government, was drafted in Philadelphia.

It met instant, violent abuse. Patrick Henry and other war heroes condemned it as an attempt to set up a new tyranny in place of the old.

At this point three leaders—Hamilton, Madison and Jay—resolved to do all in their power to urge adoption of the Constitution. Over a seven-month period they wrote sixty-five essays or letters under the pen name of Publius. These essays, known to us as the *Federalist Papers,* were published in various New York newspapers—some in the New York *Daily Advertiser*. What was their impact?

Newspapers in many towns, according to custom, freely reprinted the Publius essays. They were thus circulated in all states.

Everywhere they were read word for word. In coffee-houses they were read aloud and debated. Everywhere, debates were fed by the arguments of Publius.

In some of the state conventions the vote was close. New York's convention ratified by 30 to 27.

A series of essays, each published in a newspaper hand-printed in an edition of a few hundred copies, had made itself felt throughout the nation.

Today groups of like-minded people, wishing to urge their views on the public, likewise look to the communication media. Like our early newspapers, the mass media serve as a forum.

Let us see what is involved.

To celebrate Bill of Rights day, let us suppose the American Civil Liberties Union asks for television network time and is promised a half hour, ten thirty to eleven P.M. Three famous jurists will discuss the current significance of the Bill of Rights.

The offer of network facilities does not mean that all the stations of the network will broadcast the program. Each affiliated station will make its own decision.

Thus the problem, for the organization sponsoring the broadcast, shifts to the local scene.

A week later, the manager of a Midwest television station is trying to make a decision. Managers of scores of other stations, in other cities, are doing the same.

The manager has a choice of (1) the Bill of Rights program scheduled by the network—sure to anger some people, and also to bore some; (2) the local college basketball game with its traditional rival—sure to win a good audience but involving the expense and trouble of a gymnasium pickup; (3) an early Jack Benny movie, dated 1941, which the station has rented as part of a series and has available throughout the week—sure to anger no one and involving no trouble.

The manager is becoming increasingly Jack Benny-minded when a phone call comes from the president of a local department store, a leading advertiser. The manager takes the call.

The president mentions that he has become chairman of the local chapter of the Civil Liberties Union. He wants the manager to know that the local chapter will help publicize the scheduled Bill of Rights broadcast. The chapter had a meeting last night and resolved on a vigorous local campaign to help the station build an audience for the coming program.

A follow-up letter repeats the offer of help. On the local Civil Liberties Union letterhead the manager notes interesting names: a prominent local lawyer, a clubwoman whose husband owns two supermarkets, a local labor leader, a churchman, other influential people.

There has been no "pressure," only an offer of help. But such an offer, from the right person, is the best kind of pressure. Pressure that looks like pressure has to be resisted.

The scheduling of the broadcast by the station does not end the chapter's problems. The broadcast may have to compete with a beer-sponsored boxing match and an old Rita Hayworth movie on the other television stations; a symphony orchestra, hillbilly barn dance and disc-jockey program on radio; and various local movies and events. The effort already made may be wasted unless the program is promoted—through the local press, churches, clubs and other groups.

Even if the broadcast wins an audience, one will not be sure to what effect. Audience research, which can be expensive, may supply part of the answer.

It will be clear that the use of the mass media by citizen organizations bears little resemblance to three men sitting in their studies sending essays to the local paper under the pseudonym "Publius." The difference goes to the heart of what mass communication is.

Mass communication, in several respects, is a typical outgrowth of the Industrial Revolution.

It involves: (1) *quantity production*—of words, images, sounds; (2) *wide geographic distribution*—without which quantity production would be meaningless; (3) *retail outlets*—television station, radio station, newspaper, theater, store, library, club, church, school. Through all these outlets, mass communication woos its audience.

Mass communication, it will be noted, follows the industrial pattern in a very important respect; in words as well as clothes, we have created a buyer's market.

When cloth was scarce, so were printed words. That is

why the reader sought them out, read them hungrily, cherished them. Today clothes must find the buyer. And the word goes in search of the audience.

Once it was true that if a man built a better mousetrap, the world would beat a path to his door. Now the mousetrap beats a path to the door of the customer.

It is not enough, in our time, to mass-produce words, images and sounds, however fine and true. We must also deliver them to the customer and get him to heed them. We must take them to him in theater, school, church and club. The words must accompany him in his car and down the road. They must follow him to his supermarket, pursue him to his home. It is a buyer's market.

Within a buyer's market there may be sellers' markets, resulting from special shortages. We shall find this true in the arena of words, images, sounds.

But this does not alter the over-all historic change—the result of the rich abundance we have learned to produce.

That is why we say that the communications revolution, like many others, has had some effects in the reverse direction. What should be easier gets harder.

This presents us with a paradox. In our age of mass communication, we are for the first time thinking of communication as a problem.

For the first time we have books and courses on communication, the communication arts, communication research. Business, government agencies and citizen groups have consultants on mass communication.

And that is because successful mass communication is not only increasingly difficult, intricate, expensive. It is also increasingly important. As businesses, governments and groups grow more huge and complex, they are increasingly aware that they must communicate or perish.

BIBLIOGRAPHY: The History of Mass Communication

SELECTED READINGS

Archer, Gleason L. *History of Radio to 1926*. New York: American Historical Society. 1938.

Eder, Josef Maria. *History of Photography*. New York: Columbia University Press. 1945.

Gramling, Oliver. *AP: The Story of News*. New York: Farrar & Rinehart. 1940.

Jacobs, Lewis. *The Rise of the American Film*. New York: Harcourt, Brace. 1939.

Landry, Robert J. *This Fascinating Radio Business*. Indianapolis: Bobbs-Merrill. 1946.

Lee, Alfred McClung. *The Daily Newspaper in America*. New York: Macmillan. 1937.

Leigh, Robert D. *The Public Library in the United States: The General Report of the Public Library Inquiry*. New York: Columbia University Press. 1950.

McMurtrie, Douglas C. *The Book: The Story of Printing and Bookmaking*. New York: Oxford University Press. Rev. 1942.

Mott, Frank Luther. *American Journalism: A History of Newspapers in the United States Through 250 Years: 1690 to 1940*. New York: Macmillan. 1941.

———. *Golden Multitudes: The Story of Best Sellers in the United States*. New York: Macmillan. 1947.

———. *History of American Magazines*, 3V. Cambridge: Harvard University Press. 1938.

Newhall, Beaumont. *The History of Photography from 1839 to the Present Day*. New York: Museum of Modern Art. 1949.

Presbrey, Frank Spencer. *History and Development of Advertising*. New York: Doubleday, Doran. 1929.

Ramsaye, Terry. *A Million and One Nights*. New York: Simon and Schuster. 1926.

Rosten, Leo C. *Hollywood: The Movie Colony, The Movie Makers*. New York: Harcourt, Brace. 1941.

Rotha, Paul; with Griffith, Richard. *The Film Till Now*. New York: Funk and Wagnalls. 1950.

Schramm, Wilbur (ed.). *Communications in Modern Society*. Urbana: University of Illinois Press. 1948.

————. *Mass Communications: A Book of Readings Selected and Edited for the Institute of Communications Research*. Urbana: University of Illinois Press. 1949.

Seldes, Gilbert. *The Great Audience*. New York: The Viking Press. 1950.

Siepmann, Charles A. *Radio, Television and Society*. New York: Oxford University Press. 1950.

Sixty Years of 16 mm Film: 1923–1983. Evanston: Film Council of America. 1954.

White, Paul. *News on the Air*. New York: Harcourt, Brace. 1947.

Willis, Edgar E. *Foundations in Broadcasting: Radio and Television*. New York: Oxford University Press. 1951.

PERIODICALS

American Heritage. New York.

The Quarterly of Film, Radio and Television. Berkeley: University of California Press.

REFERENCE WORKS

Dunlap, Orrin E. Jr. *Dunlap's Radio and Television Almanac*. New York: Harper. 1951.

Smith, Bruce L.; Lasswell, Harold D.; and Casey, Ralph D. *Propaganda, Communication and Public Opinion: A Comprehensive Reference Guide*. Princeton: Princeton University Press. 1946.

The PSYCHOLOGY
of mass communication . . .

WE have traced an epic of the industrial age. It tells how men developed means for mass-producing words, images, sounds, and getting them to far-flung audiences.

The audiences so reached may be huge, or not so huge. They may include tens of millions, millions, hundreds of thousands, tens of thousands, thousands—*or hundreds*.

Those who have reached small numbers include many who hoped to reach more, and some who were trying to do exactly what they did: reach a small, specific target.

There are many good reasons for aiming at a small audience. Some of the most compelling successes of mass communication have involved highly specific audiences. Each medium has developed channels for reaching such audiences. We shall have to consider these later.

Nevertheless, the search for the huge audience dominates the field.

Of course it does. High costs make it inevitable. The needs of business make it inevitable. And it is made inevitable by the needs of the government agencies and citizen groups who turn to the mass media to reach a general public.

Some who have hoped to reach a large audience, and been disappointed, have an easy explanation of the huge-audience phenomenon. They say that huge audiences are won only through the superficial and trivial. But the history of mass communication does not bear this out.

If the New York *Journal*'s comic strips made nineteenth-century journalism history, so did the New York *Tribune*.

51

If *The Sheik* was a best seller in the 1920's, so was the substantial *Outline of History*.

If *Love Finds Andy Hardy* was a box-office success in the 1930's, so was the historical *Life of Emile Zola*.

If *Believe It Or Not* was a pocket-book best seller in the 1940's, so was the classical anthology *Pocket Book of Short Stories*.

If Jackie Gleason was a television smash hit in the 1950's, so was Maurice Evans with full-length telecasts of *Hamlet* and *Macbeth*.

The history of mass communication suggests that substance is no bar to large-scale success, and triviality no guarantee of it.

All the more reason why, in discussing the psychology of mass communication, we should begin with a look at audience pull. What makes this phenomenon? What draws and holds huge audiences? Is "entertainment" the secret?

If so, what is entertainment? And why do we call it "mere entertainment"?

A woman who has called her son eight times to leave his comic book and come to dinner; who has called her husband four times from his favorite television comedian before he gave sign of hearing; who has seen her daughter week after week spend all her allowance and sitter earnings on movies; and who has for two months, in spite of herself, been following a daytime serial while doing her housework—such a woman knows that whatever force is involved in these absorptions, it cannot be called "mere." Far from touching only the surface, it has the nature of a compulsion.

In truth, the astonishing pull of the very successful story, film, program or advertisement can hardly be explained except in terms of Freudian theory—the theory of the unconscious.

1 The Hidden Force

Freud and others have shown the part played in our lives by unconscious forces.

Early frustrations begin to shape these. Reaching for pleasures, we find them withheld. Yielding to impulses, we find them punished. "No!" is the theme song of everyone's early years.

The stifled impulses do not disappear. Unless later gratified in some way, they remain as a constant charge in the unconscious part of our minds.

Banished from our thoughts, along with the guilt feelings connected with them, they may be "forgotten." But they are still there, repressed.

This mechanism of repression is, of course, essential to individuals and society. Without it, we could not live in a social order.

But the accumulation of *imprisoned emotions,* as Freud called them, can build an enormous pressure that influences our lives—sometimes in a troublesome way. Thus repression is an adjustment mechanism that can lead to trouble.

The psychologist sees various evidences of repressed wishes. In our dreams, while the censoring conscious sleeps, wild impulses may flash to the surface. In our speech, slips of the tongue may betray hidden wishes. In our behavior, compulsive acts may show the inner pressure.

But one of the most interesting evidences of inner pressure is a mechanism by which we try to cope with it: the mechanism called *fantasy.*

It is the beginning of all the arts, including literature and drama, and of the satisfactions derived from them.

FANTASY. Every human being tries to repair the exasperation of painful episodes by re-imagining them—with revisions. In our minds we do things over and change some of the details.

In childhood this is the basis of endless pretendings which we call "play." Since the mother is the agent of many child frustrations—the main no-sayer in most homes—it is not surprising to find the child constantly pretending: "I'm the mother."

In the course of these games a young girl will visit on her dolls countless frustrations she herself has suffered. This is turn-about, frustration frustrated. It is also a path to adjustment.

Sometimes she involves others in these games. A three-year-old will tell her mother, "You be the baby." Then the game becomes complex. It proceeds relentlessly through various stages.

As the mother, exhausted from housework, rests for a moment on the couch, she finds her little girl cooing over her with a most loving-mother tone of voice. She is pretending to be tucking her mother in for the night. She whispers to her mother, "Lie still, baby." The mother, surprised at the tenderness, feels a glow of warmth and pride. But a moment later the child suddenly explodes in an uncanny mimicry of maternal fury. Stamping her foot she screams at her astonished mother, "Lie down! Don't get out of that bed! Don't you do that!" The mother winces. She wonders whether this is some cruel form of propaganda.

It is. It is many things. It is revenge, adjustment, repair of self-esteem, reconciliation, acceptance. It is coming to terms with life. It is communication.

We call it play. Perhaps it is important to pretend that it is a mere pastime. It is important to us to banish and forget the impulses stored under pressure in the unconscious. And when they thrust their way into our activities, as in these games, we must disguise their origin and importance.

Later, for the same reason, we shall speak of "mere entertainment."

Sometimes the importance of the game is concealed through fanciful settings and roles. Instead of child and mother, the game becomes one of princess and witch. It is the same game. Details are different, the emotions the same.

Thus fantasy is a mechanism through which, in slight or heavy disguise, we neutralize frustrations and release inner pressures.

It is a good mechanism if it works. But misused, it can lead to trouble. Fantasy is essential. It is hard to imagine adjustment to society without it. But in our mental hospitals are some who live in fantasy and never return. Fantasy, like repression, is neither wholly helpful nor wholly harmful.

FANTASY AND THE AUDIENCE. Many observers have traced the path by which fantasy leads to the formal arts. Most people's early creative work has a core of autobiography—it is autobiography reconstructed. It is the product of an impulse to tell but also to revise, to give order and meaning to one's life. Both fiction and nonfiction spring from these impulses.

If audiences get satisfaction from a work, it is generally because it serves a similar purpose for them.

Thus for the audience, too, the game can provide revenge, adjustment, repair of self-esteem, reconciliation, acceptance.

It should be noticed that the satisfaction comes from a tapping of imprisoned emotion, which is not easily tapped. Related to painful and forgotten incidents, it is forcefully repressed.

But when we are experiencing an exciting newspaper story,

film, television play, the *conscious* mind accepts the story as someone else's, having no connection with ourselves. Thus the guard is down. Only the *unconscious* seizes the story as its own. As in fantasying, the details do not matter to the unconscious. The unconscious habitually deals in disguises.

When we find ourselves deeply moved by a story, with an intensity we can hardly understand, it is because we have secretly accepted it as our own, *identifying* ourselves with the people in it.

Identification—this is the mechanism that taps the imprisoned emotion.

It is not surprising that this term *identification,* so important in the vocabulary of psychology, is also frequently used by the practitioners of mass communication. "Will the audience identify itself with this?" Producer, editor and writer know that this is essential, for emotional impact.

When a story or situation in any medium—whether received as news or entertainment or advertising, as fiction or nonfiction, as comedy or tragedy, as truth or falsehood— holds many people in its grip, it is emotion that is holding them. Their own emotion.

Printing press, film laboratory or television studio supplies the key that unlocks the emotion. But the audience supplies the emotion—from its hidden, pressurized reservoir.

If the people weep, it is not for the heroine but for themselves. If they laugh, it is not because the hero's tensions are being relieved, but their own.

Since this is true, it means that huge-audience successes must reflect in some way the unconscious conflicts of large numbers of people.

Let us see if we can identify some of the obsessions of mass communication and suggest their relationship to prevalent tensions.

Obsession I: Taboos

From the first year of life we learn of actions forbidden and boundary lines not to be crossed. The *don'ts* accumulate rapidly.

Every one of these creates resentment. Because the don'ts stem from the parents, the resentment is against the parents.

But these same parents are also the source of affection, food, drink, comfort. Thus the child's feelings for the parents are mixed.

If the parents' love is ample, it will help the child overcome and repress the resentment. The child identifies itself more and more with the parents and with the established order.

To the extent that the repressions are not completely successful, the stifled impulses and resentments continue to play a part in the child's life.

Soon the parents, as agents of taboo, are replaced by school teacher, policeman, boss, government. All these become the heirs of the unconscious resentments.

The unconscious has a way of lumping such figures together, filing them in accordance with their place in our emotional patterns. Thus in the successive flashes of an aggressive dream, a father may suddenly and unaccountably be replaced by a teacher, policeman, umpire, tax collector, employer.

Some people divert some of their resentments or *aggressions* into sport, hobby, work, sufficiently to remain in control of them. Others are a constant prey to their own resentments.

There is evidence that millions of people continue to chafe inwardly against the world's taboos. Their impulses to violence, and their desire to overstep boundary lines, are held in uneasy check.

Psychiatrists feel we betray this in our daily speech. "He gets away with murder," we say admiringly of a colleague. "He slays me," we say of a comedian.*

The state of tension between our hidden, lawless impulses and our society-dedicated repressions is shown by our response to these conflicts in all the media of communication.

When the New York *Sun* in 1833 began to report from the criminal courts the struggles of defendants, lawyers and judges, thousands of new readers responded. When the early movies depicted struggles between policeman and tramp, the response was again instantaneous. The introduction of crime drama to radio in the 1930's quickly found millions listening.

With whom did the audiences identify themselves?

To find an answer, let us observe the taboo obsession at work in communication. First in a children's book. It is a useful beginning because in children's books, as in children, the processes are not heavily camouflaged.

The book is *Mike and His Neighbors,* by Grace Klem.†

The hero, Mike, is a spaniel. He means well but is incorrigible. He goes into houses uninvited, pushing his way into clean kitchens and parlors. He follows children into school. Practicing retrieving, he gathers the morning newspapers from neighbors' front doors and takes them home. He steals galoshes. He goes into a butcher's shop for a piece of meat. He goes to the station and boards a commuter train. He spends a night in jail and enjoys it. In short, he is impossible. Something must be done.

---

* Bromberg, Walter, M.D. *Crime and the Mind.*
† Klem, Grace. *Mike and His Neighbors.* Garden City: Doubleday, Doran. 1941.

In the book there is a picture for each of these sins. As one reads the book to a child, one can see his eyes light up with each new transgression. The child is identifying himself satisfyingly with the sinner. In fact, the story gives him so far no other character with which to identify himself. For twenty pages the child has the delight of prying into forbidden places and taking what he wants.

The fact that the hero is a dog helps the escape of emotion. Being a dog, Mike has a special moral leeway. Identifying himself with the dog, the child audience acquires the leeway. If the hero were a human, breaking rules without special circumstances, a child might feel uneasy about the identification and reject it. The story would then cease to function. But in the guise of dog, the child can more safely enter into moral abandon.

Even so, he is developing some feeling of guilt as he approaches the twentieth page. This guilt gives the story mounting tension.

If the story ended on the series of transgressions, the child would be left with the guilt. Then the story would be an aggravation, a betrayal of carefully acquired social repressions. But of course the story doesn't end here.

Instead the spotlight shifts to the owners of the dog, Mr. and Mrs. Dobbs. We now see these nice people sitting on their front steps in despair. The story tells us: "Something had to be done."

For the first time the child is invited to experience the situation from their point of view. "It was useless to scold or to chain Mike. Long country walks tired the Dobbs but didn't tire Mike."

The boy begins to identify himself with the owners and their problem. But he still, at the same time, remains the dog. It is therefore an anxious moment when he hears: "They had almost decided to give him away . . ."

This moment is anxious because the boy is divided against himself. He has an emotional identity with each side of the conflict. He is the dog and he is the owners. Therefore it is a great relief when he learns: "They found a better solution. They had a baby, John Joseph Dobbs, Jr. From that day on, Mike was a changed dog. He no longer roamed all over town . . . he is too busy at home now. It is Mike who plays with baby when he is awake, and who guards him while he sleeps . . . he is a family dog with responsibilities."

The story has given the boy the luxury of breaking rules, and in the end the luxurious glow of social approval. He has eaten his cake and has it.

The story might be called a safety valve. But it could also be called education or propaganda, in that it fits in with society's efforts to turn a barbarous child into a civilized adult. Clearly it also serves as an extension of the child's mechanisms of adjustment, by which he tries to reconcile himself to a world that presses him with taboos.

The story shows the complex functions that hide under the word *entertainment*. A father, vaguely conscious that the story serves his purposes, is glad to provide it—to *sponsor* it, we might say. As for the child, he demands it again and again. So long as there is in him an uneasy fiend that wants to climb fences and take what he sees, so long will there be something in him that clutches at stories like this.

It should therefore not surprise us that the story is similar to thousands of others, identical in inner meaning though different in outward guise. As we grow older, we require different outward guises, trappings, details, mood, literary level.

Screen writers will recognize this as a "regeneration story." Hollywood has used countless stories in which the audience, because of special circumstances, identifies itself

with someone who turns lawbreaker, but who is finally re-
deemed. This is also a recurrent formula on such television
series as *Inner Sanctum Mysteries*. It is a favorite among
pocket-book suspense stories. In quite different mood and
disguise, all these play the same fantasy game as *Mike and
His Neighbors*. They provide the luxury of revolting against
society, and the luxury of putting down the revolt.

We find it also in *Crime and Punishment* by Dostoevski,
this time with epic proportions.

And that brings us to an important point. We have been
talking about kinds of communication that win and hold
large audiences because they deal, in a satisfying way, with
universal emotional conflicts.

When a producer senses that he has a story of this sort,
he feels sure he can please a large audience. If the story also
has literary values, he feels he can also reach a discriminat-
ing audience. The universal audience does not bar the dis-
criminating audience. It can include it.

We have seen the same pattern at work on various levels:
child level, melodrama level, Dostoevski religious level.

It also works on an advertising level. The advertiser is
not much inclined to appeal to our society-defying impulses,
but sometimes he does—as with the advertisement of the
lady who walks down the avenue in her brassière. She looks
jaunty. We might feel uneasy about it all until we are reas-
sured by the caption that it is perfectly all right: "I dreamed
I walked down Fifth Avenue in my Maidenform Bra."

The taboo obsession and its conflicting forces seem to
motivate the censorship of literature and art, as well as their
enjoyment. This may help to explain the fanaticism of some
censors.

The taboo obsession affects all kinds of people—both
sexes, all ages, all economic classes. It appears to grip the

young more strongly than the old. Some practical implications of this will appear later.

Obsession II: Omnipotence

Before birth, says Dr. Sandor Ferenczi, a child lives in a state resembling omnipotence. His every need is automatically supplied.

After birth, for a time, a feeling of omnipotence persists. Figures hover about to supply every wish. The child hardly needs to imagine what it wishes. The wish materializes.

But this illusion soon dissolves. The child must begin to signal its wants with sounds and gestures. Even this effort may prove futile. Amid periodic rages, omnipotence slips away. As the child becomes aware of its surroundings, it also learns of its own powerlessness.

There is a consolation. Among those who hover about are a few whom the child gets to know well, and they *are* omnipotent. The father, for instance, can move about anywhere, lift the child anywhere, supply countless things.

The child shares in the omnipotence of the father, which is thus a kind of guarantee that the child itself will, in time, struggle back to power. The child identifies itself with the father, imitates him. It begins a long, slow process of making itself over in the image of the father.

Years pass and the child, now a boy approaching manhood, is increasingly conscious of growing power. Every day his strength, capability and knowledge increase. There is a sense of approaching fulfillment.

But there is a betrayal. It has become clear that the father is not omnipotent after all. In fact he is not much of anything. He is a shadow having little resemblance to the all-powerful image that still lingers in the boy's mind. The

actual father is a betrayal of that image. The son unconsciously resents the father.

Meanwhile the boy's growing feeling of power, struggling
toward the hidden image, reaches its high mark in early
manhood. He becomes husband and father, and achieves a
kind of omnipotence—at least as an image in his child's mind.
That image will someday be betrayed, because the young
father is already starting a slow decline. He represses the
knowledge of it. The decline continues.

This life cycle of impotence-omnipotence forms an obsession which, like the taboo obsession, produces fantasy and
art. In all the media of mass communication we can see
this obsession at work.

We see it in the popularity of such Western figures as the
Lone Ranger and Roy Rogers. They repair the failure of all
fathers by never failing.

In these hero tales, as in taboo-obsession stories, there
are usually two or more figures with which the audience
identifies itself. For it is an inner conflict that is being played
out. The plot generally revolves around some mortal figure,
a person with a problem. This person realizes his need for
the help of someone more powerful. He accepts his mortality
and does not go in for razzle-dazzle heroism. He represents
the audience's painfully acquired acceptance of a limited
human role.

But the audience also identifies itself with the Lone
Ranger, Roy Rogers, etc. The omnipotence image in the unconscious still keeps its hold.

The Roy Rogers addict may occasionally camouflage
this by scoffing at the hero for his never-fail perfection. For
the same reason Superman addicts may scoff at Superman.

These are signs of effort to grow up. We keep trying to

repress the omnipotence image. But the image pushes its way out in new disguises. As we grow older, the disguises become more sophisticated. Instead of romantic ranges and interstellar spaces we may choose a more familiar locale, while still giving our hero remarkable, even magic powers.

Thus in the delightful film *It Happens Every Spring* a professor, who happens to be a baseball fan, discovers a fluid that repels wood. A few drops on a baseball will make the ball dart away from a swinging bat. With this secret the professor becomes, temporarily, a major-league pitcher, a scientific baseball Superman.

In much of our crime-detection fiction, we cling to the idea of omnipotence through intellect.

Omnipotence dreams are the motive power behind much advertising: for expensive cars, clothes, whiskeys, yeast tablets.

Mass communication, harnessing this powerful, repressed obsession, can create heroes overnight: in politics, journalism, entertainment. Deep within us we keep looking for a leader with whom we can merge our powerlessness and proceed to a promised land.

Thus, in 1898, the young William Randolph Hearst, crusading at the head of his *Journal,* roused millions with the feeling of destiny and world mission. In later years others did the same via radio.

But if this makes heroes fast, it can also topple them fast. Many a movie star has not questioned why suddenly twenty million people attend his movies, two hundred magazines publish his pictures, twenty thousand people write him for autographs. Perhaps he ascribes it to curly hair and hard work.

But a few years later, with his box-office value declining, he sees evidence that a number of people hate him. Strangers write him spiteful, angry letters. Columnists berate him. He asks, "What have I done to them?" The answer is, he has done nothing to earn their hatred. It is the destiny of human heroes to have feet of clay. And this is always a betrayal of secret images, unguessed even by those who hate.

The movie idol, through mass communication, has happened to become connected with the submerged hopes of millions. As long as such hopes persist, they will be betrayed.

The force of this obsession, like the taboo obsession, can be harnessed to good or evil. It lends its strength to much of the idealism of the young.

"When I was younger," said a thirteen-year-old boy questioned in a sociological study, "I used to make up stories about Superman; he always used to lick them all. Now you know one person can't win all the time. I lost interest in Superman when the war came. Real heroes, like Eisenhower, sprang up during the war and I like reading about them better." *

Obsession III: Security

We have seen how parent love fortifies a young child against early frustrations. Love eases the tensions; it reconciles, heals.

But before long the love seems to have conditions. It has trap doors. Even in the happiest families, it can suddenly switch to exasperation and rejection.

In the early years of many a child, the following incident occurs hundreds of times. This and similar incidents, and the relationship they reflect, may play an important role.

At first the problems of toilet training are accepted by the

* Wolf, Katherine M. and Fiske, Marjorie, "The Children Talk about Comics." In *Communications Research 1948–1949*. Edited by Paul F. Lazarsfeld and Frank N. Stanton.

mother with equanimity. But this soon begins to evaporate. How many two-year-old girls have come into the living room and found mother with a guest, and seen the lady's arms stretch out to welcome and hug her? "How she's grown! How pretty she is!" The girl comes forward for the embraces. But in the midst, affection freezes. There is a sudden hoarse cry of revulsion. The girl is aware of being clutched by her mother, snatched from the room with a despairing groan. At other times hugs are preceded by furtive inspection.

The child is aware that her acceptability into society is conditional. The world's love for her hangs by a thread. A trap door may give way at any moment.

When control is achieved, the child's early years disappear from memory, far beyond the reach of her conscious mind. Is it an accident that the totally "forgotten" years of childhood correspond so closely to years of constant humiliation?

The girl grows older and goes to school. On the first day she has a sudden panic. Why? She sees nothing to fear, but she feels as if she is sitting on a trap door.

Years of physical growth prepare her for new roles in life. She gets married. Just before the wedding she has another panicky time when she trembles and weeps. She does not know why.

We are all conscious that some people have obsessional needs for reassurance. All of us, in some degree, feel insecure about our place in home, office, club, community. These hidden feelings may go back to an early relationship that made constant, rigid demands—meant as discipline but experienced as threat. As life goes on, new threats draw voltage from the old. The fears merge. When our anxieties seem to mount beyond visible reason, it is because the hidden source is supplying the current.

These repressed emotions, like others we have mentioned,

produce fantasy and story. They give us tales like *Cinderella*, in which a girl is surrounded by threats: a hating stepmother and hating sisters. But against these, fantasy offers a secret source of strength—a fairy godmother.

Our security tensions often produce the fantasy of orphanhood. Is fear the cause of this? Or is it our repressed resentment of parents that makes us try out, in imagination, the state of parentlessness? Perhaps both emotions find an outlet in the theme—as in the perennial success, in various media, of *Daddy Long Legs*.

As we grow older and more knowing, the demands of intellect grow stronger. The conscious mind sees through fables. But the pressures may remain, to break through perhaps in a work like *The Grapes of Wrath*. Here the orphan has been transformed into Okies, adrift in a parentless world. Society's trap doors have opened for them.

Here the basic fantasy has been overlaid with an epic panorama, rich in realistic details. These persuade us of its truth, allowing our emotions to pour through. Our watchful intellects would not now permit us to put our hopes into a fairy godmother or a rich Daddy Long Legs. But it could be done through the sympathetic overseer of a government camp for migrants.

Our point is that whether we view such a work as literature, propaganda, sociology, it is something else too. It is a trigger mechanism that starts a chain reaction in millions of people, releasing unguessed forces. They are the power we feel in the story.

The hidden trap door, and the search for a way to lock it, play a part in entertainment, advertising, propaganda, popular songs, jokes. The security obsession sells deodorants, insurance policies, political causes, soap.

The struggle against vague feelings of insecurity is far more important to most people than the struggle against dirt. The soap advertiser knows this and tries to merge the two.

Many people can see the unconscious search for security in the success of a novel, a daytime serial, a *Peace of Soul,* but cannot see it in the work of a television comedian. Surely those who produce laughter are dealing in "mere entertainment." But the psychologist tells us that when we laugh, we are enjoying the reversal of frustration in its most compact form.

The situations of successful farce are akin to those of tragedy. A man dangling on the edge of a roof makes us howl with laughter in one film, squirm with agony in another. The emotions tapped are the same. Different moods are different aspects of disguise.

Max Eastman, in *The Enjoyment of Laughter,* analyzes brilliantly how the triumphant frustration of frustration is packed into the seconds of a joke. Before the convulsive release which we call laughter, the following takes place.

First we are led to expect something. Then, as we reach for the expected, it is snatched away and something else is substituted. So far we have retrod the familiar path of frustration.

But almost as the substitution is made, we note something. The substitute has a surprise in it, a reward. It is better, far better, than what we reached for. In the moment of frustration we are enriched. Here it is at work:

A young man goes to see his prospective father-in-law to ask for the girl's hand. He is ushered into the private study. The father invites him to sit, gives him a cigar, looks him over. Then he asks: "Well, young man, how are your financial prospects?"

The young man replies: "Very good, sir! Unless your daughter has misled me."

THE STEPS: In such a trap-door situation, involving security-insecurity, we quickly identify ourselves with the boy. With him we reach for the prize, the approval, the girl. "Very good!" brings victory in reach. Then he spoils it by hedging. But in this moment of spoiling, we spy a new prize: not only girl, but money.

In jokes, too, the pumpkin turns into a carriage.

We have reviewed some of the leading obsessions of popular films, programs, books, advertisements, jokes, in order to emphasize the following:
/ The successes of mass communication draw their power from the latent emotions of people.

They are successful on a large scale because they fit, as a key does a lock, the emotional repressions of millions. They fit the lock and are able to open it in the same way as do fantasy and childhood play.

Thus we see mass communication serving as a vast extension of the adjustment mechanism within us. Wide success, far from being explainable in terms of superficiality, must be explained in opposite terms. Deep emotions are involved.

Some people think love or sex are essential to large-audience success, but there have been many big successes without these elements. The strength of these themes lies in the fact that they bring into play simultaneously taboo obsessions, omnipotence obsessions, security obsessions. They are thus certainly among the surest routes to emotion.

Mass communication, with its physical separation of communicator from audience, appears to need the link of emotion more than does face-to-face communication. Mass communication, like other modern production-distribution industries, serves a public that is remote, unseen.

The larger and more diverse the audience, the more the

link is needed. The huge-audience press, film, radio, television, reaching out to people diverse in occupation, age, education, background, cannot win and hold them in terms of subject-matter interests. A more universal language is needed. Universal repressions provide the language.

If emotion provides the link, this does not bar material that is intellectually challenging. The universal language conveys many kinds of meaning.

The same emotions are tapped in the successes of fiction and nonfiction, comedy and tragedy. They are at work alike in entertainment, news, promotion, education, propaganda.

The tone of the communication may be calm or excited, serene or troubled. These can be merely different keys to the same locked emotions, which are unlocked by audience identification with others, real or unreal.

Wherever the mass media have won huge new audiences, it has been through communication patterns that offered emotional release through identification. So important is this phenomenon of identification that we must now consider it further.

2 Identification

We identify ourselves with others in hope of reward.

We sense, in the secret charade of identification, a chance to circumvent taboos we dare not violate, win old battles already lost, lock firmly trap doors still quivering beneath us.

In the widely successful communication, the story situation, headline or artwork generally hints of the possible reward.

Sometimes it may seem to do the opposite. Often it threatens us. Many films open with situations that threaten life and home. Advertisements threaten marriage, job, reputation. But these threats are implied invitations. We are always glad to re-experience through the identifications of art the threats that have defeated us, because we know this gives a chance to amend the defeat.

This is implied in all communication. Communication is a second chance. By communicating, we amend experience and make order out of chaos. The threats in art are invitations to the healing of wounds.

The pull of the invitation is in the relationships seen or implied. These must make a link with relationships in our lives and tensions.

If relationships make the link, what about details such as place, time, age of characters?

Many people assume that identification is strongest when there is identity of place, time and age. But there is no evidence of this. A boy in Boston can identify himself satisfactorily with a boy in Boston. But he can also identify himself with a dog, as in *Mike and His Neighbors*. Also with a Roman soldier, Eskimo, or baseball pitcher. People all over the world had no trouble identifying themselves with the Chinese farmer of *The Good Earth* and the heroine of *Forever Amber*.

Certainly, if remoteness introduces confusion, identification may be inhibited. If the audience doesn't understand why the news from Bagdad should alarm the caliph, it will soon withdraw from emotional merger with the caliph. But if details and their meaning are clear, remoteness does not hamper identification. It may help it. There are advantages in imagining ourselves remote in time and place. Unconsciously remoteness may circumvent repressions. As a lovely lady in Restoration England, we may permit ourselves actions we would not risk in present-day Albany. In the guise of a Viking explorer, we may credit ourselves with deeds we would not credit in Cincinnati.

Some people believe that identification is strongest where there is identity of social and economic status. Again evidence does not suggest this.

The armed forces long believed that a training film or orientation film should feature a soldier or sailor "to promote identification." A central character of this sort may be dictated by subject matter, but not by the needs of identification.

In testing the training film *How To Operate the Army 16 mm Projector Set,* Army researchers found something that puzzled them. Analysis of audience reactions showed that most trainees identified themselves not with the central character, a trainee, but with the instructor.* Did soldiers identify themselves with those of higher rank? This seemed at odds with official assumptions. But the history of the arts suggests that such identification is indeed possible. Most writers and directors have long assumed that Shakespeare made no serious mistake in using as central characters such figures as Prince Hamlet and Prince Hal.

There may be special advantages in the upward identification. The Theater Guild's *U. S. Steel Hour* had a play about a man who saw there was a plan afoot to edge him out of his job. He thought he was right for his job and wanted to keep it. The story showed how he went about it. The play, *The Great Chair,* happened to deal with a university president and his struggle with a Board of Trustees. The play succeeded because it was also the story of every man and his

* Hoban, Charles F. "Determinants of Audience Reaction to a Training Film." In *Audio-Visual Communication Review,* Vol. I, No. 1, Winter, 1953.

insecurity. And many a haberdashery salesman nervous about his place in the world may have derived extra pleasure from experiencing his worries in the guise of a university president.

The upgrading identification operates advantageously in many motion pictures. Through a movie, a housewife considers the problem of hanging on to a husband, and does so amid *Vogue* and *House Beautiful* trappings.

Some people believe that audiences enjoy an upgrading identification but resist a downgrading identification. Again, this is doubtful. The success of Charlie Chaplin, one of the most world-wide deliriums mass communication has produced, was built on identification with a tramp.

The downward identification seems to offer luxuries of its own. It provides outlet for self-pity more readily than does the upward identification.

If low-status heroes are outnumbered in the mass media by high-status heroes, this may be due less to audience preference than to sponsor preference. The upgrading identification is clearly more helpful to merchandising. Also, by telling us again and again that the rich are as troubled as the poor, it seems to support the established order.

The low-status hero and setting, on the other hand, make for sponsor uneasiness. They seem to put the spotlight on economic problems.

All in all, we find that the pattern of human relationships, seen or implied, makes the essential emotional link. For this purpose all other matters, such as status, age, nationality, occupation and animal species, are secondary. These may serve as valuable disguises, to divert and cajole the conscious mind and disarm repressions.

At the heart of every identification is a wish. The conflicts of drama make use of our conflicting wishes—some conscious, some unconscious.

✗ If a character behaves toward others in a way we would not wish to behave, we reject the identification.

If we must reject all sides of a situation, we withdraw from the story. If we do not take part emotionally in it, there is no story, no drama.

There must be early opportunity for identification with at least one character, or there is no story, no drama.

In discussing the role of identification, we have referred more often to dramas and novels than to commentators, analysts, speakers. Is this because drama and similar forms give greater scope for identification and emotional release? There seems no doubt that this is so. And it brings us to a fundamental problem of communication, with important implications for many kinds of sponsors.

IMITATION AND NARRATION. Centuries ago Plato said that one can tell a story in two ways: by imitation or narration. He pointed out that one can also use a combination of these.

Of the two, narration seemed to Plato far more noble. He felt that it should be preferred by virtuous men.

But he pointed out that "to children and the attendants of children and to the vulgar mass," imitation seemed preferable. Worse, they were likely to be especially pleased with imitations of ribald and wicked characters.

In the perfect state, Plato felt, it would be best to have only "austere and less fascinating" narration, and to prohibit imitation—certainly of evil.*

Thus Plato voiced alarms that have been echoed many times in subsequent ages. And he embodied the spirit of censorship in extreme form. But he was certainly right about popular preference.

* *The Republic of Plato.* Book III. Translation by John Llewelyn Davies and David James Vaughan. The word *narration* is used as film, radio and television would use it—to mean anything spoken by a narrator. It may be narrative, descriptive, expository, hortatory.

In the early Renaissance, the religious theater, like the Greek theater before it, used narration and imitation. The clergy emerged from the church and became presenters of drama. Simple human scenes depicted biblical episodes and the lives of saints. Men of the church explained their meaning. The success was great—so much so, it soon presented problems. The fall of angels was more fascinating than the explanations. Ranting Herods and other villains stole the show. Comedy bits were padded into major roles. Actors became idols. Finally, in dismay, churchmen abandoned imitation and returned to the pulpit—and austere narration.

Again let us skip centuries, to a time when every mass medium was engaged in both narration and imitation. But instead of imitation, we would say *dramatization*. In 1935, the Republican party, disturbed over the small audience rating of many broadcast orations, decided to go in for drama. In buying time for the 1936 election campaign, it informed the major networks of its decision "to take advantage now of modern radio technique to convey our message." Alarmed, the Columbia Broadcasting System and the National Broadcasting Company conferred. They notified the Republican National Committee that they would not permit dramatization. They explained, in a correctly Platonic stand:

Appeals to the electorate should be intellectual and not based on emotion, passion or prejudice. We recognize that even the oratorical discussion of campaign issues can be to a degree stamped with the aforementioned flaws, but we are convinced that dramatizations would throw the radio campaign almost wholly over to the emotional side. Then, too, we believe that the dramatic method by its very nature would tend to over-emphasize incidents of minor importance and significance, simply because of dramatic value. . . . The turn of national issues might well depend on the skill of warring dramatists rather than on the merits of the issue debated.*

Because local stations did not adopt the network policy, the National Committee was able to broadcast dramatic recordings. In following campaigns the jingle, the dramatized spot announcement and the animated cartoon crept into broadcast politics. The trend toward combining narration and dramatization continued—always against opposition.

The incident shows that we, like Plato, feel uneasy about the dramatic method and the emotion it can unleash. We do not like to think of its influencing decisions. We think of emotion as a delinquent, a repeated offender, who is best locked up.

Freud gave us a somewhat different picture.

It is true that he saw the unconscious as a prison for rejected wishes, rejected as unacceptable. But these wishes, he said, might be directed toward new ends. Like other mechanisms of adjustment, this can have good or bad results. If impulses are successfully transferred to socially acceptable ends, Freud called the process *sublimation*.

Thus Freud saw the prison also as a powerhouse, providing the driving force for great crusades. He saw man's hope in the redirecting, not the banishing of inner drives.

John Dewey, writing of education, held a similar view. He saw the problem of education as the channeling of inner desires toward meaningful goals.

Teachers who did not want to think about students' inner desires but only about the subject matter to be taught were warned by Dewey that "underlying desires determine the main course of thought." A teacher might well wish to

* *Political Broadcasts.* A series of letters exchanged between the Columbia Broadcasting System, Inc., and the Republican National Committee. New York: Columbia Broadcasting System, Inc. 1936.

abolish them. "But they are not abolished; they are not suspended; they are not suppressed—save with reference to the task in question. They follow their own chaotic and undisciplined course." *

On the other hand, once the inner forces have been focused, the mind is propelled toward learning. It seizes information, shapes ideas. The mind learns because it wants to.

Now we have come, by a long route, to the role of information and ideas. If we have been a long time in reaching these, it is not that we considered them unimportant in mass communication. Rather, their importance could not be fully discussed except in context of the deep-seated drives.

Later chapters will consider the use of the mass media by varied sponsors for varied purposes: entertainment, news, promotion, education, propaganda. All these purposes involve the channeling of repressed wishes—toward information, ideas, actions.

Let us now examine this channeling process. We shall observe, step by step, what we shall call the *communication cycle*.

Channeling process of Communicat

3 The Communication Cycle

The cycle includes: *expectation, attention, emotion, information, idea, action.*

(1) *Expectation.* A mass-produced communication nears its audience: viewer, reader, listener. He may be at home, in a car, in a theater, or elsewhere.

Regardless of what the content of his unconscious may be, he has at the moment a set of feelings and expectations which are at or near the surface and can play an immediate

* Dewey, John. *Democracy and Education.*

role in the receiving of a communication. This role is obvious in one's experience with face-to-face communication.

Suppose you are a young man driving through the neighborhood of a girl friend. She has a cute figure and nice legs, and you know that she owns a yellow hat.

Presently a yellow hat appears around a distant corner. At once you see vividly the cute figure and the legs.

Presently the woman nears. Now you see that, though she wears a yellow hat, she is scrawny, middle-aged, and has no figure.

What you saw was partly *perceived* and partly, as the psychologist says, *apperceived*. One small part of the vision came around the corner, the other part from your own expectant mind.

This phenomenon is a constant factor in communication.

When the 1938 Orson Welles broadcast of *The War of the Worlds* caused hundreds in the New York area to leave homes, pack cars and flee, the reaction was certainly influenced by expectations. It was the year Hitler precipitated the Munich crisis. Day by day, radios had brought news of international threats and the mobilizing of nations. To many people war seemed near. Welles' Martian invasion was only an extension of expectations.

Thus the hopes and fears of the moment play a part in what we see and hear. They can transform its meaning.

If this is a hazard to face-to-face communication, it is even more so to mass communication.

In face-to-face communication, the communicator has some idea of the state of mind he must deal with. He can even influence it. The Fuller Brush man at the door sees whether the housewife is calm or agitated and proceeds accordingly. Lecturer, preacher, theater actor vary performance according to audience. In mass-produced, mass-distributed communication this is impossible.

The mass media do have some remedies. These include the broadcaster's advance tune-in announcements, newspaper listings, newspaper advertisements. These build audiences but also help shape their expectations. Wrong expectations can boomerang.

In printed media, expectations are conditioned by titles, artwork, typography, format, and what the reader knows about publisher, author, illustrator. Here too, misconditioning can boomerang.

The motion-picture field has experienced many such boomerangs. A story about a lonely eight-year-old girl, whose parents tried to stop her dream-world imaginings and thus complicated her emotional problems, was mistitled *The Curse of the Cat People*.

The title was meant as box-office stimulant but created expectation of weird and supernatural events. Poster artwork did likewise. The false expectation miscolored the audience's entire experience of a tender and penetrating film.

In the 16-mm motion-picture field, serving audience units which often discuss as well as watch, a reliable remedy is available. Preliminary comment can condition expectation. Closed-circuit television and radio programs, and programs broadcast to classrooms, offer similar opportunities for preparation.

An example will show how important such preparation can be.

All My Babies, a brilliant documentary film, was made for the training of midwives in Southern states. Many Southern children are delivered by midwives. Through the film, midwives with many decades of experience learn new medical practices.

The film follows a Southern midwife through her work with several cases—one in detail. The midwife and family who helped make the film, permitting the presence of two cameramen during delivery, did so in a spirit of dedication. They were helping the cause of healthier babies everywhere. This fact is generally explained to the midwife audiences.

Midwives are traditionally religious. The work they do is regarded as a sacred trust. All this is shown in the film.

The first groups seeing the film were deeply moved. As a result the details of correct midwifery, as shown in the film, seemed indelibly impressed on the women's minds.

But after successful showing with a number of classes, one class reacted unfavorably. Deep hostility seemed to sweep through the group. When time came for discussion, they sat in silent anger. The supervising nurse was at a loss.

Finally she realized: she had forgotten the usual opening explanation. The midwives, not knowing how the events of the film had been made visible to them, experienced them as a desecration. Matters of sacred intimacy had by some trick been revealed on a screen. Indignation transformed the experience.

After this incident, explanations were never omitted and hostile reactions did not recur.

Such danger is generally smallest with specialized audiences. The writer of an article or advertisement for a trade paper knows whom he is addressing. Films for specialized audiences have this same advantage. Yet even here, as we see, expectations may distort.

The help that face-to-face communication can provide at this point, when mass communication is at a disadvantage, can be important.

Thus every communication is conditioned by the fact that it is received:

In a particular state of feeling and expectation . . .

(2) *Attention.* The quest for attention, as we saw in our short history of mass communication, has become increasingly competitive. This results from the abundance we have created. It has two consequences:

(a) Increasing sensationalism in artwork, headlines, sound effects, musical effects, book covers and other devices for securing initial attention.

(b) Decreasing impact of these same devices.

The search for the arresting effect, to secure attention, has a way of pursuing itself in circles. Norman Corwin wisely observed, "Sometimes you can attract attention by being relaxed."

To hold as well as win attention, it is important to realize that the essence of full attention is not surprise, which is momentary, but something else: *participation.* The audience is held firmly only when it is *doing.*

This active role may involve picture-making. A cartoon of a politician may stimulate by giving only the line of his jaw— nothing else. The audience is made to supply the rest.

The role may involve puzzle-solving. A headline or title or opening sentence may pose a provocative question: What caused the Kremlin shift? Who is the Washington mystery man?

The role may involve plot-making. We see a young lady, in darkness, digging a hole in the garden with a big spade, and we begin to plot: "She's hiding a body."

But each of these examples involves more than the participation of picture-making, puzzle-solving or plotting. Each begins to involve also the participation of feelings. And this is the strongest hold.

Attention may be thought of as an amplifier in the mind. Signals from the world, no matter how shrill, will have little impact unless the amplifier is brought into the circuit. The amplifier will light up if the signals touch, even lightly, the buttons marked *hoping* and *fearing*.

So far the steps in our cycle are:

> *In a particular state of feeling and expectation*
> *Certain incoming signals ignite our attention . . .*

(3) *Emotion.* Active attention has prepared us for the tapping of deeper emotion.

In the first step of the cycle, in the conditioning of expectation, narration was helpful. But now we find far more value in dramatization—showing instead of telling.

In the identifications of drama, we shed the oppression of our identity. We stop being ourselves. Narration, on the other hand, usually insists that we be ourselves. There is less chance of escape.

Of course dramatization—showing—may tap little emotion when it only shows someone telling. And narration—telling—may from its circumstances have the emotional effect of showing.

But while the dividing line between them is blurred, this does not affect the principle: emotion yields more readily to dramatization than to narration.

In the earliest stage of our cycle, we found mass communication at a disadvantage in comparison with face-to-face communication. But in the present stage, mass communication holds every advantage. Separated from communicator, the audience is spared confrontation. Confrontation holds us to our identity, tunes every repression to full pitch. The mass media, on the other hand, preserve privacy. They do so in the chair at home or in the darkness of the theater. The identifications of drama can have full scope.

These inner identifications, as we have seen, lead to a dilemma. The audience is maneuvered into a crisis. Deeply buried impulses drive it to resolve that crisis.

The involvement of these unconscious forces heightens the mind for the next stage.

Our cycle thus far:

> *In a particular state of feeling and expectation*
> *Certain incoming signals ignite our attention,*
> *Then tap our hidden power lines of emotion,*
> *Stepping up the voltage of . . .*

(*4*) *Information.* At all stages of the cycle, information plays a part. But now the mind, driven in a quest, experiences heightened activity. Now relevant information from the mind's storehouse is amplified and brought into play. Now also the mind has intensified power to seize new information.

Nothing is more unassimilable than gratuitous information unrelated to needs or wants. Nothing is more easily assimilated than needed, wanted information.

If the advertisement, artwork and headline have done their job, the reader will read the important copy because he wants to and needs to.

If the newspaper headline, lead, illustration, have done their job, the reader will read the later facts because he wants them and needs them.

If the opening scenes of the documentary film have done their job, the audience will seize the later information because it wants it and needs it.

Information plays a part in all entertainment, in all media, at all stages. But the writer knows he dares not give the important information until the audience wants it and needs it.

An audience of the like-minded, whose inner drives are already focused in a common direction, makes for a swift communication cycle. The route *expectation-attention-emotion-information* can then be traveled in a matter of seconds. But the same elements are involved.

The information that crosses the gap between communicator and audience—via paper, film, wire, air—is grasped and remembered only if it serves needs and wants. The most insistent needs and wants, as we have seen, are those which stem from childhood and grow into unconscious obsessions. Driven by these, the mind not only seizes information but also forms ideas.

(5) *Idea.* Implicit or explicit ideas play a part in all communication. A communication of tight structure, like a play, story, article, cartoon, song, advertising message, usually has a dominant idea. An idea in this sense is a doctrine, belief, principle, often expressible in a sentence.

Most people feel their actions are determined by their ideas. On the other hand, cynics feel that people's ideas are changed to fit their emotions and actions.

Actually pressure seems to be applied in both directions. Thus ideas are part of the machinery by which we hold in tentative equilibrium the forces inside us.

The most powerful impulses to action are unconscious emotional drives. Yet we do not readily permit ourselves actions not sanctioned by our announced ideas. Thus attempts to influence action usually aim at two levels: the idea level and the emotion level.

We may hold contradictory ideas. In matters of dispute we believe: "Compromise is a good thing." We also believe: "Give them an inch and they'll take a mile." A crisis may lend special urgency to one of these ideas and strengthen its place in our mind. The crises we experience through mass communication, by identification with others real or unreal, may have the same effect.

The relation of emotion to idea has been compared to a river and its banks. The river is a mighty force, the bank a mere pattern of influences. The river may force changes in the pattern. Yet the pattern steers the river on its way.

The cycle thus far:

> *In a particular state of feeling and expectation*
> *Certain incoming signals ignite our attention,*
> *Then tap our hidden power lines of emotion,*
> *Stepping up the voltage of related information*
> *And impelling us to the formation of an idea,*
> *Thereby driving us toward . . .*

(6) *Action.* The drives awakened in mass communication demand expression through action. Throughout the cycle nervous impulses travel through the body, preparing it for action.

We see it in young television viewers. They perspire and jitter. After the cowboy film they pounce on each other and start pummeling.

The effectiveness of training films is based on this phenomenon. Identification starts glands and muscles working, demanding action.

Some communications demand the action of talk. "Great books," said A. Whitney Griswold, "require great conversation to complete their meaning."

Laughter and tears are other ways in which meanings are completed through action.

Immediate action not only satisfies, but clinches the effects of communication. This has application in all kinds of mass communication.

If a man uses the coupon in the advertisement, he is more likely to remember the advertisement and what is said. A jolt to unconscious feelings may not be remembered. But if it produces immediate conscious activity, it probably will be remembered.

Immediate discussion of information and ideas roots them more firmly. Film forums, Great Books discussion groups, and the use of broadcasts in the classroom as discussion springboards, are applications of this principle to educational ends.

Discussion as a clincher plays an important part in propaganda. In the Soviet Union "personal oral agitation," highly organized, is reportedly used to supplement mass communication. At film sessions and broadcast listening groups, trained "oral agitators" launch the discussion.*

The role of café and saloon in the rise of various mass media may have been more important than appears at first glance. It provided talk as a clincher.

The immediate clinching action, whether talk or deed, may be only an intermediate goal. But this may, through new cycles, lead to other actions and ultimate goals.

In the first stage of our cycle, we found face-to-face communication important. In this final stage, we once more find mass communication dependent on face-to-face communication. What is said and done, between people, now intensifies or moderates the impact. The identifications of drama are gone now. We are ourselves again.

The final effect of a politician's broadcast prophecy of doom may depend on what a father says or how he raises his eyebrow in the family circle.

The final effect of an advertisement may depend on what a salesman says or does, at the door or in a store.

* Inkeles, Alex. *Op. cit.*

This suggests that mass communication is not so much an end in itself as something that feeds face-to-face communication. The final effect of mass communication is seldom accomplished directly. Its main effect is generally through the talk and action it sets in motion.

It is powerful because it can cause many people, in many parts of the country, to discuss and do the same things at the same time. This may start ripples which reinforce each other, gaining momentum. Most large successes of mass communication must be explained in terms of this snowballing, indirect effect.

This view of mass communication has many implications. It explains why the mass media have not replaced the peddler, as some thought they would. Instead, according to the National Association of Direct Selling Companies, there are more door-to-door salesmen than ever before—approximately a million. Mass communication has become their foot in the door. Without it they are at a disadvantage. However, it cannot do their work.

The same thing applies to teachers. Some have urged investments in educational television on the grounds that proportionately fewer teachers will be needed.* This is a shaky, dangerous assumption. Television, like films, radio, printed materials, should be thought of as a powerful feeder of the classroom. Without the mass media, teacher and student cannot adequately deal with a world of growing complexity. But the mass media cannot do the teacher's work.

The same thing applies in politics. The nationwide broadcast can give added zest and meaning to local meetings. It cannot replace them.

We have found that communication pushes us toward

* See, for example, "TV Can Solve Our Educational Problems," New York *Times* Magazine, Dec. 19, 1954.

action, and is successful to the extent that it produces action. Some actions are more difficult to obtain than others. For some actions, greater resistance must be overcome. The greater the resistance, the more the need for face-to-face communication.

We have seen that *entertainment, news, promotion, education, propaganda* have much in common. All channel emotion toward ideas and actions. But in the *kinds* of actions sought, they vary. They vary, too, in the resistance they must overcome.

Entertainment channels our emotions toward a reinforcement of accepted ideas. There is immediate emotional reward in reduction of tension. The final action is renewed acceptance. There is little resistance.

News puts the emphasis on information—theoretically, of any new happening. But principles of "news value" emphasize events which touch emotion and invite identification. According to one editor, news is what makes people say, "Gee whiz!" News, in this sense, offers immediate emotional rewards. A more ambitious news policy may meet slightly more resistance.

Promotion puts the emphasis on the final action. It channels our emotions toward certain products or services. There may be resistance. But if the rewards are clear, if the product or service involves no conflict with accepted ideas, the resistance may not be great.

Education pushes us, via long-term action, toward distant goals. It channels our emotions toward a continued organized quest for information and ideas. Because the rewards may not be immediate, rechanneling of powerful drives is needed to overcome the resistance.

Propaganda pushes us toward acceptance of new ideas and behavior. Resistance may be powerful.

Thus we see that different kinds of communication, aiming at different ends, must overcome very different degrees of resistance. In general, we have listed them in order of increasing difficulty. But these divisions must not be thought of as neatly separate compartments. The terms overlap. To some degree all communication is entertainment, news, promotion, education and propaganda. All pursue the same cycles.

CYCLES WITHIN CYCLES. The cycle of communication, as we have described it, may be seen in clear form in many short communications, such as television commercials.

In a longer communication, like a novel or feature film, we have cycles within cycles. Many times during a novel there is new effort to seize attention, tap deeper emotion, harness it to new information, stimulate a new idea—all the ideas leading to the final climactic idea. Such cumulative cycles can reach the deepest emotions.

There may also be interrupted cycles, as in serialized fiction, or a book read in separate sessions. A cycle can apparently be suspended and resumed, with little relation to other cycles. The television play that is interrupted for the commercial does not heighten with its emotion the facts of the commercial. The commercial must launch its own cycle. It may inherit, from the play, a large audience and a helpful state of mind. But the commercial must itself tap the emotion it needs.

We mentioned that in dealing with special audiences, already focused on special interests, the communication cycle can be shortened. We suggested that for such an audience, the steps *expectation-attention-emotion* can be telescoped.

This needs some elaboration. What makes an audience *focused?*

In advertising, can you afford a near miss?

COMMUNICATION CYCLE—EXAMPLE. Reading an advertising trade publication, our . . . (1) *expectation* is of institutional advertising, tending to be pompous. This advertisement therefore attracts our . . . (2) *attention* by its jaunty manner. This attention is re-enforced by a jolt to . . . (3) *emotion* because of gruesome content. The jauntiness is important now because it disarms repressions. Since all is in fun, we let ourselves enjoy the murderous moment. Of course, we would not enjoy it at all were it not for the fact that something inside us finds the head a more attractive target than the apple. This stifled inner force, getting momentary release, adds voltage to the . . . (4) *information* that Young & Rubicam, Inc. prepared this advertisement, and impels us to form the . . . (5) *idea* that Young & Rubicam is an excellent advertising agency, and pushes us further to the . . . (6) *action* of dropping the advertisement casually on the desk of an office friend and asking, "What do you think of this?" He looks at it, starting a cycle of his own. His consequent action is necessarily somewhat different from ours. He nods his head and says: "Conscience." When this puzzles us, he explains: "This was clearly the work of a brilliant advertising man, who like many advertising men is a little uneasy about advertising. Here, in the disguise of comedy, a truth slips out: that we must often aim a little lower than we pretend—straight for the unconscious." This starts some talk in the office. The advertisement is remembered especially because it set up ripples of face-to-face communication.

4 Focused and Unfocused

As a young man grows up today in the United States, he finds around him countless invitations to identification. These include family, teachers, school heroes. They also include thousands of mass-produced, mass-distributed heroes.

For a while, in obedience to strong obsessions, he is likely to attach himself to a film-television-radio-cartoon cowboy. But as he matures, the cowboy's triumphs seem to be more and more a repetitive ritual. Annoyed with its hold over him, he looks elsewhere.

He meanwhile merges himself with, let us say, the Cleveland Indians. This brings moments of unutterable exhilaration, leading always to frustration. This too is a merry-go-round, a trap. He keeps searching—he is not sure for what. He watches boxing bouts and is an easy prey for murder mysteries.

Meanwhile his school grades are mostly C. But one A-minus—in Shop—leads to an uncle giving him a tilting-arbor power saw for Christmas.

The power saw becomes a source of prestige. Neighborhood kids come in to look at it. The boy makes some Christmas presents for relatives and these arouse admiration.

One summer he works at a gas station and sells some of his carpentry products by the roadside. For the next summer he makes a deal with the gas-station owner. He sets up shop behind the station. For hours each day he turns out nests of tables. By the time he is a college junior he has two students working for him during summer vacation and clears seven hundred dollars.

He has always been a slow reader but some subjects now seem easier. He gets A's in engineering. In a business course, he suddenly develops strong interest in the practices of manufacturers, wholesalers, jobbers and retailers. Economics, dull at first, develops interest when it gets to the subject of bank loans. A few years later he has a small manufacturing plant with five employees. He gets married.

Marriage is an outlet for many kinds of drives. So is business. He is in fierce competition with another small business near by. In the middle of the night he thinks up new counter-moves. He cannot conceive that he once lay awake thinking up victories of Indians over Yankees.

He becomes vice president of a local business club. Once a great consumer of advertised hair tonics and shaving lotions, he hardly notices their advertisements now and does not know the names of new brands which his son is using.

He reads few novels. But he finds he can get through a huge volume of reading. Whipping through the morning paper, he takes cognizance of several dozen matters. Ever since he began importing African wood he has had interest in African affairs, currency exchange rates, tariff policies, shipping problems, State Department policies. At the office he gets through twelve trade papers.

He and his family are interested in many things, many information media. A growing number of subjects has acquired meaning for him. But he hates articles which begin with silly human-interest stories apparently designed to motivate you. He wants immediate facts.

This does not mean there is no emotion in his quest for facts. Rather, his stored-under-pressure impulses have found their channels—rewarding outlets for aggressions, power needs, security needs. His mind is always ready to seize information. He is a focused audience.

In the focused audience, drives have been processed into "interest" in business, public affairs, hobbies.

The serving of such audiences through newspapers, trade papers, newscasts, information films, is not one of the difficult problems of communication. It is not a matter of stirring emotion. It is not a matter of bringing it into new focus. It is a matter of satisfying emotions already focused.

It is therefore a kind of communication that requires little dramatization. It can often do its job with narration. It is therefore not the most expensive kind of communication.

All in all, mass communication for the focused audience is done with skill and thoroughness. In the United States those in search of information can find it in abundance. When they begin their search, they are often astonished to find the information so close at hand. They ask, "Why didn't I know about all this?"

But these people are not the real problem of mass communication. They are not the people who make up the huge audiences of television, radio, film, press. The huge audiences are the unfocused, in search of focus.

THE UNFOCUSED. This is the audience that represents the challenge to mass communication.

Many decades ago John Dewey observed the following: The gap between the capacities of the newborn and what we expect of the adult grows wider and wider. The problem of bringing each new screaming infant up to scratch grows more and more difficult. Today the gap is still widening. The young experience this as pressure.

As the world grows more crowded and complicated, its taboos also multiply. The young experience this as pressure.

As the world grows more urbanized, and the dangers and demands of frontier and country life recede, an outlet for pressure is gone. The pressure mounts.

As the world grows more industrialized, fewer people seem

to find in their work an outlet for pressures. Competition between companies does not mean competition on the assembly line. The assembly line is mechanical, impersonal. It may heighten the pressures.

Beneath them a huge force is held in restraint. It is searching for direction.

Who will give it direction? What aims will possess the unpossessed?

This great inner force is pulled this way and that way.

Every year billions of dollars are spent on publications, films, broadcasts, to give direction to this force. In this struggle for the American mind, tens of thousands of organizations are involved.

We shall examine the work of these organizations. But first let us look at the tools they use: the media.

BIBLIOGRAPHY: The Psychology of Mass Communication

SELECTED READINGS

Allport, Gordon W.; and Postman, Leo. *The Psychology of Rumor*. New York: Henry Holt. 1947.

Bromberg, Walter, M.D. *Crime and the Mind*. Philadelphia: Lippincott. 1948.

Bryson, Lyman (ed.). *The Communication of Ideas*. New York: Harper. 1948.

Cantril, Hadley. *The Invasion from Mars*. Princeton: Princeton University Press. 1940.

Cantril, Hadley; and Allport, Gordon. *The Psychology of Radio*. New York: Harper. 1935.

Charters, W. W. *Motion Pictures and Youth*. New York: Macmillan. 1933.

Dewey, John. *Democracy and Education.* New York: Macmillan. 1916.

Doob, Leonard W. *Public Opinion and Propaganda.* New York: Henry Holt. 1948.

Freud, Sigmund. *A General Introduction to Psychoanalysis.* New York: Boni and Liveright. 1924.

―――. *Psychopathology of Everyday Life.* New York: Macmillan. 1951.

Hovland, Carl I.; Lumsdaine, Arthur A.; and Sheffield, Fred D. *Experiments on Mass Communication.* Princeton: Princeton University Press. 1949.

Katz, Elihu; and Lazarsfeld, Paul F. *Personal Influence: The Part Played by People in the Flow of Mass Communications.* Glencoe, Ill.: The Free Press. 1955.

Lazarsfeld, Paul F.; and Stanton, Frank N. (ed.). *Communications Research 1948–1949.* New York: Harper. 1949.

――― and ―――. *Radio Research 1941.* New York: Duell, Sloan and Pearce. 1941.

――― and ―――. *Radio Research 1942–1943.* New York: Duell, Sloan and Pearce. 1944.

Lippmann, Walter. *Public Opinion.* New York: Harcourt, Brace. 1922.

Merton, Robert K.; Fisk, Marjorie; and Curtis, Alberta. *Mass Persuasion: The Social Psychology of a War Bond Drive.* New York: Harper. 1946.

Riesman, David; Glazer, Nathan; and Denney, Reuel. *The Lonely Crowd.* New Haven: Yale University Press. 1950.

Ruesch, Jurgen, M.D.; and Bateson, Gregory. *Communication: The Social Matrix of Psychiatry,* New York: Norton. 1951.

Schramm, Wilbur. *The Processes and Effects of Mass Communications.* Urbana: University of Illinois Press. 1954.

Smith, George Horsley. *Motivation Research in Advertising and Marketing.* New York: McGraw-Hill. 1954.

Wiener, Norbert. *The Human Use of Human Beings: Cybernetics and Society.* Boston: Houghton Mifflin. 1950.

PERIODICALS

Audio-Visual Communication Review. Washington: Department of Audio-Visual Instruction, National Education Association.

Public Opinion Quarterly. Princeton: School of Public and International Affairs.

REFERENCE WORK

Cantril, Hadley (ed.). *Public Opinion 1935–1946*. Princeton: Princeton University Press. 1951.

The MEDIA
of mass communication . . .

EACH medium arrived in a series of explosions.

Each aroused hope and anger. Each saw the rapid growth of a device into an industry. Each developed heroes and heroines who won admiration and trust. Each became available, as a channel of influence, to business, government, citizen organizations. Each showed power over men's minds.

We now see that the power was, in each case, the same power. It was not in the medium but in the submerged impulses of men and women. The medium tapped these—it did not create them. The same power source was available to all.

But though the source was the same, methods differed. Each medium was found to have its own abilities and weaknesses. Each developed its own characteristics and its own organizations.

We turn now to a study of these characteristics and organizations.

1 The Printed Page

As an instrument for touching human emotion and influencing thought and behavior, the printed page has one outstanding weakness—which is also its strength. This is a paradox we shall meet, in different form, in each of the media.

The printed page, alone among mass media, does not have the human voice. Thus it lacks an element from which film, radio and television derive warmth and impact. The film industry went to huge effort to acquire the human voice. Print lacks it.

But at second glance, the weakness is strength. The printed page is the one medium in which the audience sets tempo. The reader is not controlled by voice tempo. He can race ahead, or stop to savor. He can go back or skip.

For the unfocused audience these advantages may be slight. For focused audiences they are everything. To the focused audience, the tyranny of tempo is exasperating. If for no other reason, the printed page will always remain for the focused audience the chief source of information.

There is another weakness that is strength. Print, when it relies on words, asks more of its audience than any other medium.

First it demands reading effort. Many people, because of emotional blocks, physical defects or inadequate training, find this effort great.

It also demands constant imagining. Readers who cannot meet this need, because of limited experience or capacity, may drop by the way. But for those not eliminated, the heightened participation is the special pleasure of reading. They enjoy a book in proportion to their participation.

The power of poetry is based on this. Poet and reader play a game. The game is to see how intense an experience can arise from the fewest words. The more the reader contributes, the better.

For this reason alone, the printed page seems likely to remain a chief source of pleasure for the sharpened mind.

There is one more weakness that is strength. In a government-sponsored conference on books, a 4-H club girl member said, "Going to a movie is a conventional dating habit, but who ever heard of a couple staying home to read a book?" *

For the unfocused, the restless, tugged by hidden drives looking for direction, this is a serious liability. For the focused audience it is a blessing. At the same time, the privacy of reading does not exclude later discussion "to complete its meaning."

The printed page, for many reasons, is the preferred medium of the focused audience.

During its first few centuries, the printing press served such an audience and no other. Even at the time of the American Revolution, as we have seen, books and newsletters from the hand-powered presses served a thin stratum of the population: those trained for leadership or risen to it.

Serving such an audience, the press saw no reason to seize attention and motivate readers. The audience sought the word. Writing style reflected this. Plato might have called it "austere narration." It seldom dramatized.

But in the 1830's the press began to reach for new, unfocused audiences. Almost all the changes which, since that time, have helped to make the printed page a huge-audience medium, have been in the nature of dramatization.

The court reporting in the *Sun* brought to newspapers increased use of dialogue. The stories tried to give the reader the sensation of actual experience. Then came the high-pressure news coverage of the *Herald*. Stories *"By Telegraph!"* from distant places made the reader a participant in world events.

Presently wood engravings, sometimes based on daguerreotypes, began to appear in magazines. Inviting emotional identification, they helped the rapid growth of magazines.

* Stefferud, Alfred (ed.). *The Wonderful World of Books.*

Never Underestimate the Power of a Woman!

At mid-century newspapers were gripping the emotions with headlines. By the end of the century banner headlines screamed across the page.

The earnest or fiery crusades of a Horace Greeley, Joseph Pulitzer or William Randolph Hearst invited powerful identification. It was reader and editor against an evil world.

The sob-sister columns, sport features, and other entertainment elements that became prominent in journalism in the late nineteenth century, all offered outlets for emotion through identification.

Even more important in this respect were the cartoon, which led to comic strip and comic book; and direct reproduction of photographs, which led to rotogravure section, picture newspaper, picture magazine, picture book, with all their ability to dramatize action, conflict, crime, glamor, adventure. Planned in terms of *close-up, long shot, over-the-shoulder shot, reaction shot,* they are closer to film than to printed language. They call for visual storytelling. In them we find the role of art director becoming as important as that of editor or writer—sometimes more important. The art director or designer has become a key figure in advertising,

---

DRAMATIZATION VIA PRINTED PAGE. This advertisement shows the growing role of the art director or designer in the strategy of printed communication. The advertisement was *written;* but more importantly, it was *designed.* The design relied on the satisfaction of audience participation. The communication had little meaning unless one recalled that a woman had, for the first time, been appointed Assistant Secretary of Defense. This act of recall would not be merely a stimulating intellectual exercise. For many women it would also be an act of pride. Unconsciously, the *Ladies' Home Journal* would become associated with this feeling of womanly pride.

magazine publishing, even book publishing: guiding expectation, seizing attention, planning the attack on emotion.

When print addresses a focused, special-interest audience, these dramatizing techniques are less important. But they have helped print hold its own against film and television as a huge-audience medium.

Of course print has, in comparison to these, a weakness. Or is it a weakness? In film and television, figures move. Millions of man hours of research made this possible. The moving figures of people, it has been assumed, are the main assets of these media. And no doubt they are.

But the principal asset of the still picture is: it does not move. Here only, the smile and the wind-blown skirt are frozen in time. They can be studied, cut out, discussed, pinned up, kept for later moments, filed. Free of imposed tempos, the reader decides.

VERSATILITY OF THE PRESS. Serving a vast range of purposes, the press has constantly increased its technical versatility. It has processes, papers, inks for countless purposes.

In organization, the world of print includes many realms: books, periodicals, display media—as well as pamphlets, leaflets and similar forms, distributed by mail and through company racks. Each of the major realms has its subdivisions.

Books are published by (1) *trade publishers,* selling through two thousand bookstores and a few other stores; (2) *paperback publishers,* selling through some two hundred thousand outlets, including newsstands, cigar stores, drugstores, supermarkets; (3) *textbook publishers,* selling through schools and colleges; (4) *religious publishers,* selling through churches and church schools; (5) *university presses,* selling through bookstores and direct to special-interest readers; (6) *book clubs,* selling by subscription and distributing by mail; (7) *comic-book publishers,* selling mainly through newsstands—and perhaps properly classified among periodical publishers. Some companies operate in several of these categories. It will be noticed that each category involves its own system of distribution. Each has its own economic basis.

Periodicals include (1) about two thousand *daily newspapers,* (2) ten thousand *weekly newspapers,* (3) five hundred *general magazines,* and thousands of (4) *trade periodicals* and (5) *company publications.* These last two groups can convey a message to almost any specific target: drug salesmen, manufacturers of coin machines, vase collectors, Chevrolet owners.

Display media include: (1) *posters,* (2) *car cards,* (3) *counter cards,* (4) *calendars,* (5) *match folders* and other media. Again, each division has different outlets and distribution systems. Each is larger and more complex than is generally supposed. According to the Match Industry Information Bureau, for example, three hundred thousand American business firms, one out of thirteen, distribute messages on match covers. And one company selling calendars and other forms of "remembrance advertising" to local businesses throughout the United States, Brown & Bigelow, markets them through more than a thousand field representatives at an annual volume of approximately fifty million dollars.

Sponsors. The various divisions we have mentioned all depend, at least in part, on the support of sponsors: business, government, organizations. During the past century and a half the degree of dependence on sponsors has increased.

The role of sponsors is clear enough in the fields of periodicals and display media, less clear in the case of books. But here too sponsors have become important. A book may be made possible by a business firm, government agency, or

Class. 22—General Editorial

LIFE

A Time Inc., Publication

Provides Circulation Statement subject to audit verification by Audit Bureau of Circulation.

Published weekly by Time, Inc., Time and Life Bldg., Rockefeller Center, New York 20, N. Y., Judson 6-1212.

PERSONNEL

Publisher—Andrew Heiskell.
Advertising Director—Clay Buckhout.
Assistant Advertising Director—H. Ford Perine.
Advertising Manager—John F. Morrissy.
Associate Advertising Manager—W. Dickinson Wilson.
Eastern Advertising Manager—W. C. Richardson.
Central Advertising Manager—Robin Morton.
Western Adv. Manager—C. W. Hanson (Chicago)
Pacific Coast Adv. Manager—William D. Grafton (Los Angeles)

REPRESENTATIVES

New York 20—V. J. Brosnahan, Time & Life Bldg., Rockefeller Center, Judson 6-1212.
Chicago 1—F. L. Redpath, Mgr., 221 N. LaSalle St., Andover 3-2860.
Detroit 2—John St. Clair, Fisher Bldg., Trinity 5-1212.
Philadelphia 2—Malcolm Scott, Girard Trust Bldg., Locust 8-1212.
Los Angeles 17—W. D. Grafton, 900 Wilshire Blvd., Madison 5-2101.
San Francisco 4—H. W. Markward, Shell Bldg., Yukon 2-5000.
Cleveland 15—Maurice Tompkins, Hanna Bldg., Superiod 1-1212.
Minneapolis 2—Roy Lord, Rand Tower, Main 7449.
St. Louis 3—James Dunn, Shell Bldg., Geneva 6-1212.
Boston 16—Shedd Vandenberg, Statler Bldg., Liberty 2-1212.
Atlanta 3—Tom-Chris Allen, Rhodes-Haverty Bldg., Walnut 9233.

MAILING INSTRUCTIONS

Forward all copy and cuts to Production Department of Life, 330 E. 22nd St., Chicago 16, Ill.
Send contracts for space to Life Advertising Department, Time and Life Bldg., Rockefeller Center, New York 20, N. Y.

COMMISSION AND CASH DISCOUNT

15% of gross to agencies; 2% of net 10 days from billing date. Bills rendered 20th of publication month. Cash discount for payment on or before that date.

ADVERTISING RATES

Rates effective January 16, 1956 issue. (Card No. 26.) Card received June 6, 1955.

GENERAL

Orders beyond 13 weeks at rates then prevailing. Advertising schedules composed of mixed space units are entitled to standard discounts except when the use of the smaller units lowers the total cost of the campaign below the amount which the larger units reached at their earned rate.

RATES	1 ti.	13 ti.	26 ti.	39 ti.	52 ti.
1 pg.	21,775.00	20,905.00	20,035.00	19,595.00	19,160.00
1/2 pg.	11,770.00	11,300.00	10,830.00	10,595.00	10,360.00
1/4 pg.	6,100.00	5,855.00	5,610.00	5,490.00	5,370.00
1/8 pg.	3,105.00	2,980.00	2,855.00	2,795.00	2,730.00
Agate line	41.95				

Black and white pages and spread closing two weeks preceding the date of publication, accepted at unit rate plus 10%.
All units less than 84 lines to column must be multiples of 14 agate lines at the line rate of 41.95 and a discount of 4% will be allowed on the 13-time contracts, 8% discount on 26-time contracts, 10% on 39-time contracts, 12% on 52-time contracts.
Non-standard size space in excess of 84 lines to column is charged at standard unit (i.e., eighth or quarter page) rate up to 84 lines to column and at the line rate for additional space.

COVERS (4-color process)

2nd cov.	32,740.00	31,430.00	30,120.00	29,465.00	28,810.00
3rd cov.	32,740.00	31,430.00	30,120.00	29,465.00	28,810.00
4th cov.	42,480.00	40,780.00	39,080.00	38,230.00	37,380.00

COLORS (Black and one color)

1 pg.	26,695.00	25,625.00	24,560.00	24,025.00	23,490.00
1/2 pg.	14,415.00	13,840.00	13,260.00	12,975.00	12,685.00
1/4 pg.	7,900.00	7,585.00	7,270.00	7,110.00	6,950.00

Metallic inks—rates and specifications on request.
Limited number of black and one color columns acceptable.

LOOK

Provides Circulation Statement subject to verification by Audit Bureau of Circula

Published every other week by Cowles Maga Inc., 488 Madison Ave., New York 22, N. Y., ray Hill 8-0300.

PERSONNEL

Pres. & Ed.—Gardner Cowles.
General Manager—Marvin C. Whatmore.
Publisher—Vernon C. Myers.
Advertising Director—Donald Perkins.
Advertising Manager—C. S. Hanson.
Production Director—Merrill H. Clough.
Production Manager—Charles C. Moffat.

REPRESENTATIVES

New York Advertising Manager—D. C. Howell, Bldg., 488 Madison Ave., Murray Hill 8-0300.
Chicago Advertising Manager—Fred Bauer, 33 Michigan Ave., Central 6-8127.
Detroit Advertising Manager—Phil F. De Beau General Motors Bldg., Trinity 5-2786.
Minneapolis Advertising Manager—Joseph Ba Northwestern Bank Bldg., 620 Marquette Geneva 1367.
Cleveland Advertising Manager — Ralph J. N Bulkley Bldg., Main 1-3698.
Philadelphia Advertising Mgr.—Frank T. McF 12 S. 12th St., Market 7-2587.
West Coast Advertising Manager—Vernon J. And 5858 Wilshire Blvd., Los Angeles 36, Calif., ster 3-8191.

MAILING INSTRUCTIONS

Send orders to Look Magazine, Look Bldg., Madison Ave., New York 22, N. Y. (Murray 8-0300.)
Send all copy and plates to Look Magazine, Bldg., 488 Madison Ave., New York 22, N. Y if more convenient, to Look Magazine, 330 E. St., Chicago 16, Ill. Vic. 2-1050.

COMMISSION AND CASH DISCOUNT

15% to recognized agencies if remittances are by discount date; 2% of net if remittances mailed on or before 10th of month following pub tion date of ad as printed on front cover. Bills dered on 20th of month of publication.

ADVERTISING RATES

Rates effective January 10, 1956 issue (Card No Card received July 5, 1955.

GENERAL

Rates are effective with issue dated January 10, All orders must specify whether advertising is reproduced by letterpress or gravure. The same apply for both letterpress and gravure.
Letterpress—Available in all standard unit siz Gravure—Available in all standard unit sizes e covers and center spread.

RATES

STANDARD UNITS (Monotone)

	1 ti.	13 ti.	26 ti.	39 ti.	52
1 pg.	15,065.00	14,690.00	14,310.00	13,935.00	13,5
1/2 pg.	8,430.00	8,220.00	8,010.00	7,800.00	7,5
1/4 pg.	4,295.00	4,190.00	4,080.00	3,975.00	3,8
1/8 pg.	2,210.00	2,155.00	2,100.00	2,045.00	1,9

Special rates for greater frequency and continui insertions available from the publisher upon rec Advertising schedules composed of mixed sta space units are entitled to standard discounts e when use of the smaller units lowers the total of the campaign below the amount which the l units reached at their earned rate.
To earn frequency insertion discount, schedule o sertions must be completed within the contract or less. The contract year is 26 consecutive i within one year of date of first insertion.
Two full pages facing (spread) count as two 1 tions toward earning a frequency insertion disc
NON-STANDARD MONOTONE UNITS
Single column ads less than 84 lines are at the rate of 30.12 per agate line. Single column a more than 84 lines take 1/8 page rates for fir lines and the flat line rate for additional s Double column ads of more than 1/4 page but than 1/2 page, take 1/4 page rates for first 168 and the line rate for additional space. All standard monotone units must be multiples of 14 lines.

COVERS

2nd or 3rd covers—no extra charge. See rates for units.

	1 ti.	13 ti.	26 ti.	39 ti.	52
4th cover (4 colors)	29,400.00	28,665.00	27,930.00	27,195.00	26,4

COLORS

Four colors:

1 pg.	22,640.00	22,075.00	21,510.00	20,940.00	20,3
1/2 pg.	13,415.00	13,080.00	12,745.00	12,410.00	12,0

One color and black:

	1 pg.	18,985.00	18,510.00	18,035.00	17,560.00	17,0
	1 ti.	13 ti.	26 ti.	39 ti.	5
1/2 pg.	10,475.00	10,215.00	9,950.00	9,690.00	9,4
1/4 pg.	6,215.00	6,060.00	5,905.00	5,750.00	5,5

organization through: (1) a grant to a writer, to assist in preparation of a book; (2) a grant to a publisher, to assist in publication of a book; (3) an advance order for copies. Such subsidies can play a part in any kind of publishing.

The growing role of the sponsor, in all media, will be considered in our section on *The SPONSORS of mass communication*.

Controls: Printed Page

CENSORS. If the importance of the sponsor has grown, that of the censor has declined. We refer here to the official censor.

In a sense the official censor as a controlling force in communication has been replaced by sponsors, pressure groups and media self-censorship.

There are, of course, a number of government restraints. Although the First Amendment guarantees press freedom in apparently absolute terms ("Congress shall make no law . . . abridging the freedom . . . of the press"), the application of it has never been absolute. Congress has many duties stated in absolute terms, and sometimes these con-

---

SPONSOR SUPPORT. The page opposite shows that an advertiser in *Life* is likely to pay, for a single page, between $20,000 and $40,000. If this is the value of the advertising space, how much is a picture story worth? It is not surprising that public-relations representatives far and wide are constantly developing ideas for possible *Life* or *Look* picture stories involving their clients. Page reproduced, with permission, from *Consumer Magazine Rates and Data*, one of the periodical publications by which Standard Rate and Data Service, Inc., keeps advertisers and their agencies informed about media.

flict with each other. Thus abridgements of press freedom have been introduced in the interest of the common defense and of the general welfare. Those that have been upheld in the courts have most often dealt with seditious and obscene material. Restraints of this sort have been introduced into federal post-office regulations and customs regulations. In many states and cities, similar restraints are administered by police.

When we remember the deep, conflicting impulses and repressions brought into play in communication, it is not surprising that a post office or customs or police censor can become confused by his task. Contemplating flagrant sin on the printed page, he may see it as only right and proper to outlaw it. If this misses the whole point of what story-telling is and the part it plays in our lives, the censor at least has distinguished precedents to point to. These include Plato, who felt that Homer's work would not be suitable for the perfect state because of the evil examples it provided.

All this has led, in the not-too-distant past, to such actions as the following: *

Lysistrata, by Aristophanes, was for a time banned for importation into the United States under customs regulations. Meanwhile it was read in college literature courses and had a production on Broadway. The ban was eventually (1930) dropped.

Candide, by Voltaire, and catalogues listing it, were banned (1929) from the mails. The book was meanwhile read and studied in many schools. The ban was eventually dropped.

Ulysses, by James Joyce, was for a time banned for importation under customs regulations. The ban was overruled (1933) in court action.

An American Tragedy, by Theodore Dreiser, was banned

* Haight, Anne Lyon. *Banned Books.*

(1930) from bookshops in Boston, while it was required reading in a Harvard class across the river.

Copies of *Life* magazine, with a series of pictures on "The Birth of a Baby," were seized (1938) in New York City by order of the District Attorney. In a test case, the editor was arrested. He was acquitted.

All the above censorship actions were on grounds of obscenity. All were dropped or were reversed in court. The incidents suggest the psychological, as well as the legal, complexity of the censorship problem. They also suggest the importance of the courts as a bulwark against unjustified restraints.

Court defense actions have tended to place increasingly strict limits on the area of government censorship.

TRAFFIC REGULATIONS. There are other government restraints which are sometimes called censorship, but are more in the nature of traffic regulations.

For example, the Bourne Publicity Law of 1912 introduced the requirement that paid-for advertising must be identified as such. It was criticized at the time as an invasion of press freedom. But far from stifling information, it called for additional information which provided the public with useful protection.

In a similar category are the many state laws based on a model statute originally drafted by *Printers' Ink,* making false advertising a misdemeanor. These have introduced no censorship but have made the advertiser responsible for the statements he publishes.

In somewhat the same category are libel laws. Also state laws relating to the relatively new doctrine of *invasion of privacy,* under which a person's likeness may not be used for advertising, entertainment or propaganda without his consent.

In the same category are laws under which the Federal

Trade Commission restrains unfair competitive practices; also laws under which it can restrain false and misleading advertising after hearings.

In the same category are various extensions of copyright law that have been made necessary by the expansion of mass communication. They define the relative rights of creators, publishers and users of literary and artistic material.

In the same category belong antitrust actions to halt trends toward communication monopoly. These include the action which, since 1945, has required the Associated Press to make its services available to all willing to pay for them. Previously a member newspaper could veto service to a local competitor.

None of these stifle communication. They aim at its orderly traffic. They aim at removal of road blocks. They umpire disputes that endanger traffic flow.

OTHER GOVERNMENT RESTRAINTS. Many government agencies are sponsors of communication: they publish pamphlets, subsidize books, co-operate on articles, issue releases, hold press conferences, and occasionally advertise. At first glance these activities may seem unrelated to "restraints." Yet sponsorship has an unavoidable element of censorship. The sponsor announces or withholds. However good his reasons, they may look like censorship. This problem, along with other problems of sponsorship, will be considered in our section on *The SPONSORS of mass communication.*

OTHER RESTRAINTS. Of all the stories in the annals of censorship, the one most often recounted by newspaper publishers is that of John Peter Zenger. It is mentioned and re-told in editorials, features, speeches.

Zenger, in 1734, published criticisms of the Royal Governor and was imprisoned for libel. In his trial he offered to submit proof of the truth of his statements but was not permitted to do so. Nevertheless the jury ruled for Zenger—in defiance of the court's instructions. This victory, more than any other event, made possible the guarantee of press freedom in the First Amendment.

Zenger's story was a momentous turning point. Yet the constant emphasis on it is puzzling. Is there, in the United States today, any sign of publishers being imprisoned for criticising officials? Are editors afraid to castigate governors, senators, presidents? Do they show restraint in doing so?

The questions may help put the situation in perspective. The United States press of today, like every mass-production industry, is surrounded by traffic regulations. But these regulations, which protect the press as well as the public, leave it free to say almost anything it wishes. Our press has a freedom from government censorship to be found nowhere else in the world. On the whole, we have been true to Zenger.

But the Zenger story has other elements of interest.

John Peter Zenger, in addition to publishing his paper, was its writer, editor, printer, business manager and distributor. Think of the tangle of organizations that have replaced this one man, and the interrelationships and pressures they involve! We mean relationships with trade associations, codes, unions, guilds, advertisers, advertising agencies, investors, supply sources, news sources, syndicates, pressure groups.

If a modern publisher likes to identify himself with John Peter Zenger, the impulse may involve nostalgia for a simpler world in which the censor was one clearly identifiable villain, a Royal Governor at whom one might shake a fist, and not countless small restraints from hundreds of sources.

To understand this point clearly, one must understand the industrial transition through which the press has gone. The newspaper field illustrates this transition most clearly.

The Great Transition: Press

In the beginning one man, with an apprentice or two, might run a paper. It served one community, from which it received: (1) contributions—essays, news items; (2) advertisements—often want ads. The relationships:

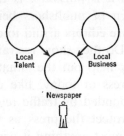

But presently telegraph wires stretched everywhere and newspapers began to have remote correspondents, telegraphing news. It was clearly senseless for thousands of correspondents to be duplicating each other in effort and telegraph expenses. Money could be saved, efficiency increased, through business combinations.

These took several forms. One was the chain: the joining of papers by purchase or merger.

CHAIN. The first chain was the Scripps chain, which started in the late nineteenth century. Later came the Hearst chain and others.

Huge savings were made. Except for local news coverage, all chain papers could be served by one news-gathering staff.

Staffs could be strengthened. In the competition for outstanding writers, chains could bid high.

At first the advantages of chains seemed overwhelming. Some people foresaw chains of hundreds of papers. Some feared the trend but felt it inevitable. Meanwhile, other cost-sharing mechanisms were developing.

PRESS ASSOCIATION. In 1848, six New York City newspapers had organized the Associated Press, as a device for sharing the cost of telegraphed news. Each paper remained independent but was served by the jointly formed organization. Similar associations developed in other parts of the country. In 1893 various associations combined to form the modern Associated Press. Today it serves thousands of newspapers throughout the world. The United Press and International News Service perform similar services.

From AP, UP, INS or a combination of them a newspaper gets news by wire, usually over a printer-telegraph machine which automatically raps out the news in capital letters on long sheets of paper. The typewritten material can be torn off as received, for rewriting or editing by the local paper.

```
UP38
   NIGHT
   SUEZ, EGYPT, FEB. 14--(UP)--SWIRLING SANDSTORMS FORCED A
STOPPAGE OF SHIPPING THROUGH THE SUEZ CANAL TODAY.
   THE FLYING SAND CAUSED POOR VISIBILITY IN THE WATERWAY AREA.
ONLY TWO TANKERS MANAGED TO GROPE THEIR WAY THROUGH.  THE REST OF
THE SHIPS IN TRANSIT THEN ANCHORED TO AWAIT IMPROVEMENT IN THE WEATHER.
   HG1225P
```

```
UP39
   NIGHT
   ISTANBUL, TURKEY, FEB. 14--(UP)--FIRE HAS DESTROYED 800 OF THE
1,400 HOUSES IN GERZE ON TURKEY'S BLACK SEA COAST, AUTHORITIES
REPORTED TODAY.  AT LEAST FIVE PERSONS WERE INJURED.
   OFFICIALS SAID THE FIRE BEGAN IN A GROUP OF OIL TANKS AND
SPREAD QUICKLY THROUGH THE AREA.
   HG1226P
```

UNITED PRESS BULLETIN. This is the form in which news bulletins from all over the world come spilling out of machines in the offices of newspapers buying the UP service.

A more recent invention allows the telegraphed impulses to be fed, via a punched tape, into the newspaper's linotype machine, automatically setting the news in type. The press associations also provide news photos, likewise by wire.

The associations result in a high degree of standardization. News stories and photos appear in exactly the same form in countless papers. This is often a theme of criticism against the associations. But it made survival possible for many independent papers. Served by huge associations, many have maintained their existence, free to pursue their own editorial policies and local news services. Some use this opportunity well, others do not. But absorption of almost all papers into huge chains would have been inevitable without press associations—and syndicates.

SYNDICATES. The syndicate provides the newspaper with features on the same cost-spreading basis. From syndicates a paper can buy, for local use, series of comic strips, political cartoons, picture stories, news analyses, sport commentaries, short stories, serialized novels, poems, advice columns, puzzles, jokes—even editorials.

Syndicates offer whole Sunday magazine sections, to which the local paper can add its own name.

Most features are supplied to the newspaper by mail. Some features, like special sections, arrive fully printed on newsprint. Others arrive in mimeographed or printed form, to be reset by the paper. Others, such as cartoons and photographs, may arrive in the form of a *mat:* a papier-mâché form or matrix in which the newspaper can pour molten metal to make a printing plate. Some features arrive in the form of metal plates.

The press associations and syndicates, so varied and complete, have to some extent counteracted the original impulse to chain operation. They offer similar economic advantage, without affecting local independence.

Chains are still being formed, now generally on a regional basis, spreading even close-to-home news-gathering costs over a number of papers. Chains, like independent papers, can buy syndicated features and press-association services.

THE NEWSPAPER AS RETAIL OUTLET. It will be clear that press associations and syndicates have changed the nature of the average newspaper. Just as a supermarket may be locally owned, yet stock its shelves with standard products, so a locally owned newspaper may stock its pages with a mass-produced abundance of standard items.

The supermarket still buys strawberries and lettuce from local farmers and performs other local services. These services are highly important, giving the store its best chance to develop individuality.

Just so the newspaper, served by associations and syndicates, has a local-service opportunity. Its long-term hope may lie in seizing this opportunity. Yet the standardized, mass-produced services provide economic backbone.

PRODUCER. Syndicates are distributing devices. A feature may be produced by the syndicate itself or bought elsewhere, for distribution by the syndicate. Thus we must distinguish between the distributing and producing units.

The producer of a syndicated feature may be a book publisher, magazine publisher, film-animation firm or other organization. Over two hundred organizations produce material for syndication.

Such an independent producing unit can sell material to chains as well as to syndicates.

Dispatches and pictures distributed by press associations may, similarly, originate with outside units: newspapers, overseas agencies.

In such cases, it is the producing unit that engages writers, artists and other services. These may be part of the producer's organization or may in turn be independent units.

Thus we find the world of print developing on three levels: *production, distribution, outlet:*

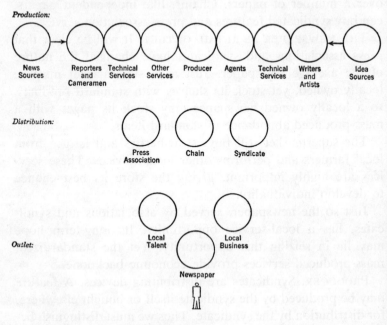

Production:

| News Sources | Reporters and Cameramen | Technical Services | Other Services | Producer | Agents | Technical Services | Writers and Artists | Idea Sources |

Distribution:

Press Association   Chain   Syndicate

Outlet:

Local Talent   Local Business

Newspaper

We must now add other levels.

We have seen that advertising began locally but became national through industrial growth. A local paper, to share in the campaigns of large companies, had to do business with *advertising agencies,* generally located in New York, Chicago and other large centers.

The chains, centrally organized, were in a good position to deal with advertising agencies. The small independent paper was at first at a disadvantage.

NEWSPAPER REPRESENTATIVE. To deal with the advertising agencies and solicit advertising from them, papers began to appoint sales representatives in large centers. A newspaper sales representative with offices in four or five cities might simultaneously serve a hundred or more different papers.

Thus national advertising began to reach newspapers via three different routes:

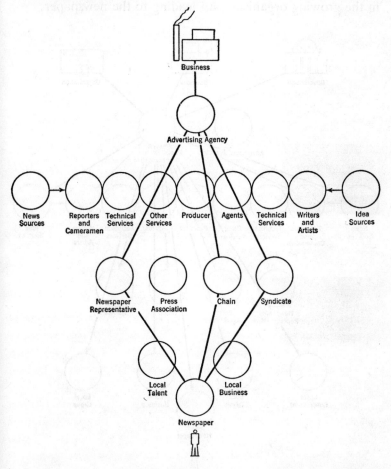

PUBLIC RELATIONS REPRESENTATIVE. We saw that as newspapers grew in influence, their content began to be a matter of active interest to many. A steady stream of news announcements began to reach newspapers from businesses, government agencies, organizations—often via *public relations representatives.** These may be employes or independent agents. Their efforts may be directed to almost any point in the growing organism—all leading to the newspaper:

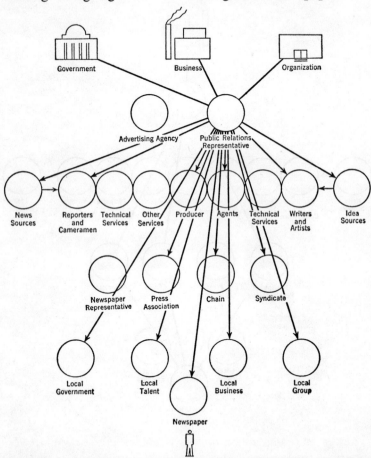

* *Public relations* is an elastic term. At some companies, the Vice President for Public Relations supervises advertising. We use the narrower meaning—not including advertising.

Our chart symbols are functions, which may or may not be performed by separate companies. Successful companies tend to assume many functions. The Hearst organization is active in those here shaded:

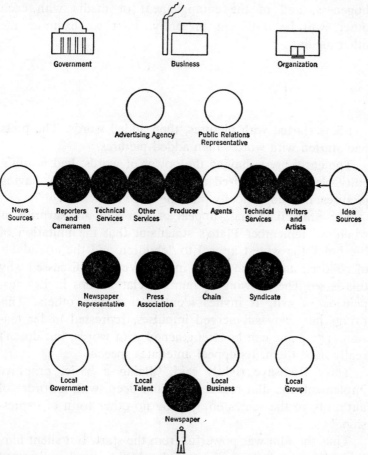

That is, it owns *newspapers;* is their sales *representative;* operates them as a *chain;* operates a *press association* (INS); *syndicates* features (King Features); *produces* them, performing such *technical services* as engraving, mat-making, etcetera. In other fields, Hearst interests publish magazines, operate broadcasting stations, and serve theaters through Hearst Metrotone News. The implications of this hugeness, and of the entanglement of media with each other, will be discussed presently. First we examine the other media.

2 Film

Films started with pictures, then added words. The press had started with words, then added pictures.

The early press, having the power of words, had no difficulty pleasing specialized audiences. The silent film, having pictures, had no difficulty pleasing huge audiences.

The immediate mass appeal of film will not surprise us when we remember Plato's statement that the imitation of life holds the widest appeal to "children and the attendants of children and to the vulgar mass." We have discussed why this is so. The showing of human relationships invites suspension of self. It invites identification with others. This brings into play submerged impulses, repressed under tension. The game can be strengthened with words, but doesn't really need them. Its appeal antedates speech.

Terry Ramsaye rightly said, "Being a basic, primitive implement, the film reaches low and deep, with an order of authority to the senses enjoyed by no other form of expression."

Thus the film was powerful from the start. But silent film, limited in words to the cramped subtitle, was handicapped in dealing with ideas. When it acquired speech, it greatly increased its importance as a special-audience medium. But the addition of speech also brought problems.

ACTION VERSUS SPEECH. In a battle for attention between action and words, words cannot win. Therefore action, with its hold on the unconscious, must be allowed to lead the way.

Words can bring powerful support to action, clarifying it and completing its meaning. But when words strike out on their own, and become busy purveyors of information and ideas not inherent in the action, then film defeats itself.

When words offer information not already *wanted* by the audience, the words are noise. When words express an idea not already being formed by the audience and crying for confirmation, the words are noise.

Information and ideas, we have seen, play a part in all kinds of communication. But they are especially important in films for news, promotion, education, propaganda. And in these, overeagerness to be informative may be especially disastrous.

In films aimed at these goals the most suitable sound track, for economic and other reasons, is often *off-screen narration*, also known as *voice-over narration*. Such narration can be very successful, but its first rule of conduct should be: "Don't go off on your own."

Meaningful action rivets the attention. It creates tensions and dilemmas in the audience. The audience inwardly asks questions. Narration should answer unspoken questions.

The questions and answers lead to an idea, gradually taking shape in the audience. The idea struggles for completion. Narration can supply words to help the crystallization. For the audience this is recognition, fulfillment.

The chattering sound track is an enemy of information. The mind shuts it out like a nagging fly.

WEAKNESS IS STRENGTH. Film, like press, found strength in its weakness.

Early movie makers soon saw themselves as no mere

novelty peddlers but storytellers, makers of drama. But could they rival flesh-and-blood drama?

At first, worrying about their separation from the audience, movie makers tried to serve that audience exactly as a play would. Whole plays and scenes, it will be recalled, were shot at a fixed distance, from a fixed point. Like a theater audience, the camera always had the entire set in view. Actors, as in the theater, faced or half faced the audience. Scenes began with entrances and ended with exits.

Hoping for the power of flesh-and-blood theater, the early movie makers merely contracted its weakness: immobility.

Then they began to discover things. Many of these discoveries are associated with the name of Griffith.

First came the shifting viewpoint. After shooting part of a scene from one angle, Griffith shot part from another. His associates worried. Wouldn't the audience get dizzy? Would it stand for these frenzied, impossible shifts? But the audience seemed to settle easily into the omnipresent role.

Then came another step. In the middle of a scene, Griffith jumped to a close-up. Again, associates were alarmed. Wasn't it contrary to nature? Besides, the close-up suddenly eliminated everything else from view. Would the audience resent this?

The audience did not resent it. And it showed no anxiety over being released from the physical limitations of humanity. It accepted readily a new, mobile audience role: watching first from one side, then from another; from far away, then from near; over the hero's shoulder, then over the heroine's; from his eyes, then from hers; from the floor, then from the ceiling; out of the window from the room, then into the window from outdoors.

In a short time the whole conception of movie making changed. In weakness—the absence of the audience—the film found mobility. From this have flowed many kinds of strength.

Film making has become the construction of a carefully calculated succession of *shots*. Shots are the building units of film.

Every shot can be charged with meaning. It can be meaningful in what it shows and in what it omits. Each act of selection can be a comment. The inclusion or exclusion of characters in a shot can suggest relationships, create inferences.

Being able to rivet attention on either speaker or listener, film can add new dimensions and meanings to dialogue.

Props and sets can acquire an active role. A new shot of the man at the desk shows, in the foreground, a woman's glove and a key. They have been there right along, but not previously emphasized. What is their significance?

The shot of the girl lets us see in the background, on the wall, the portrait of her father. What is his influence in the situation?

Thus sets and furnishings, no longer mere backdrops to action, can enter and leave the spotlight like characters.

Film is sometimes criticized as making audiences passive. On the contrary, shifting viewpoints involve the audience in constant activity.

When the film was all long shot, meanings had to be shoveled at the audience. Large gestures and expressions were needed.

Today film relies heavily on audience participation. At the height of a crisis, the close-up shows the hero's face almost motionless. The slightest muscle spasm seems overwhelmingly meaningful, not because of what it says but because of what the audience is saying.

Many crises that an audience finds brilliantly acted are

brilliant and satisfying because the audience acts them: because a series of shots, rich in implication, has so involved it in inner turmoil that it seizes meaning from the merest twitch of lip.

Thus we see film as a medium which, dealing in the essence of drama, rapidly enlists emotion.

We see it further as a medium which, by exploiting the absence of the audience, has learned to intensify its emotional power. The intensification is rooted in its ability to shift viewpoint and distance.

It can do these things not only through variety of shots, but by movement within a shot: *pan*—sideward rotation of camera; *tilt*—upward or downward swivel of camera; *dolly*—movement of camera on a wheeled mount; *crane shot*—use of camera on a large, counterweighted boom, for various altitude effects.

These devices are all tools for emphasis and implication. They can involve the audience in constant activity of thinking and feeling.

Thus the power of unspoken emphasis becomes an outstanding element in the film medium.

Words necessarily say one thing at a time. Pictures can say and at the same time imply. Combining words and richly detailed pictures, film has unique power to add, to any statement, implication on implication.

In its use of sound—dialogue, music, sound effects—film extends this power of implication through selection.

Its sound effects can be inclusive or selective. In a street scene it can use a naturalistic mixture of sounds, or it can spotlight a significant sound: a particular footstep, a baby's cry.

Music offers a similar range of choice. Music can underline the meaning of some element in the scene, or it can inject meanings not present in action or words. It can comment: satirize, deplore, encourage. It can foreshadow and remind.

The sound track is often a mixture of dialogue, sound effects, music. By control of relative volumes, the film maker can shift emphasis from one to another. Again selection is implication.

Through its flexibility in the use of sound of all kinds, film increases its ability to add implication on implication to its central statement. All this makes the audience an intense participant.

TECHNICAL COMPLEXITY. All we have said about film will suggest the complexity and expense of its production problems.

Most professional films, including those distributed only in 16 mm form, are shot in 35 mm. This does not hold true of 16 mm color films, which are generally shot in 16 mm. Whether a film is shot in 35 mm or 16 mm, there are high expenditures in equipment, personnel, materials.

For a feature film a director, in studio or on location, directs the filming of hundreds of shots. Some of these may be redone dozens of times, so that the editor will later have many *takes* to choose from. The material filmed may total ten or twenty times the length of the final feature—sometimes more.

The shots taken will vary in length from a few seconds to a few minutes. The shots of longer duration are likely to be those involving camera movement.

A moving shot can often do the normal work of several shots. A moving shot may be especially valuable near the start of a scene, unfolding situation elements one by one, while suggesting relationships between them.

In the studio, even the briefest scene may take hours to

60. MEDIUM LONG SHOT George,   (MUSIC)
    helping Alice into row-
    boat, which rocks pre-   ALICE: (SCREAMS)
    cariously.

61. CLOSE-UP Alice, terrified.   (MUSIC)
    She clings to George.

62. MEDIUM SHOT boatkeeper,   (MUSIC)
    looking off.

63. LONG SHOT George, assist-   (MUSIC)
    ing Alice into boat. Boat-
    keeper enters and starts
    to untie it. Alice sits
    down timidly.

64. MEDIUM SHOT Alice in boat.   (MUSIC)
    George, tipped in, gets
    in.

65. CLOSE SHOT George, as he   (MUSIC)
    sits down, and boatkeeper,
    untying boat. George picks   GEORGE: This boat doesn't
    up oar and inserts it   leak, does it?
    in oarlock.
                                 BOATKEEPER: I don't rent
                                 leaky boats.

66. MEDIUM SHOT Alice and   (MUSIC)
    George. He picks up other
    oar.   ALICE: Don't worry, my
                                 husband's a very good
                                 swimmer.

67. CLOSE SHOT George, reacting,   (MUSIC)
    and boatkeeper. George
    puts oar in oarlock. Boat-
    keeper shoves boat off and
    stands up.

shoot. A segment of action may be shot from several angles, each at several distances. To the film cameraman, each variation in angle or distance calls for restudy of lights, new search for expressive highlights and shadings.

The demands of the medium have encouraged specialization. Unionization has furthered this trend. Studio hierarchies of producer, associate producer, assistant to the producer, director, assistant director, cameraman, assistant cameraman, electrician, assistant electrician, boom man, mixer, property man, assistant property man, grip, assistant grip—these hierarchies lead to rigid divisions of duty. This often makes for efficiency, sometimes for waste.

As the film is shot, each day's work is speeded to the laboratory. Next day, or shortly thereafter, *rushes* or *dailies* are reviewed by director and others to see if retakes are needed. These may be ordered because of deficiencies in camera work, lighting, acting, direction, laboratory work.

Gradually the film moves, in thousands of takes, to the editor in the cutting room.

The newly shot material may be amplified with *stock footage* from a footage library: scenic shots, historic events.

The editor now has pictures on film—24 pictures per

FILM SCRIPT, in final form, shows multi-shot construction. Content of each shot is indicated. Excerpt suggests manner in which varying angles, distances, groupings, stir audience inferences and fears. Final two-column form of script is logical in film medium, in which picture and sound have separate physical existence, to be combined in final stages of production process. Excerpt is from *A Place in the Sun,* Paramount Pictures film based on Theodore Dreiser's *An American Tragedy.* As produced by George Stevens, the two-hour film has 741 shots. Average shot length: 9½ seconds.

second of projection, 1440 pictures per minute—and sound, which has generally been recorded on separate tape.*

He begins combining material into a *rough assembly*. This requires two parallel operations, picture and sound, which he must keep in synchronization. His editing equipment helps him to do this.

Studying material available for a scene, he may try a particular succession because it seems to:

> *Tell the action most clearly*
> *Make strongest impact*
> *Have most beauty*
> *Avoid heroine's occasional hard look*
> *Flow most smoothly*

He also edits for tempo. He knows that a series of short, staccato shots can quicken the pulse. Shots of longer duration are more relaxing. In his editing, he gropes for an appropriate rhythm.

Lagging actions may be telescoped. The defeat of the old baseball pitcher has been dramatized by filming: the disastrous pitch, the swing and crack of the bat, the soaring home run, the screaming crowd, the relief pitcher starting from the bull pen, the old pitcher leaving the field, the old pitcher turning on his shower bath.

The editor may cut this to:

(1) Old pitcher throws ball
(2) Bat swings and wallops ball as crowd screams
(3) Pitcher turns on shower bath

* For newsreels and similar material *single-system* cameras may be used. In these, picture and sound go directly onto one strip of film. This limits the possibilities of editing. Also, it requires sound track and picture to have the same laboratory processing—not desirable from a technical point of view.

Meanwhile climactic moments may be stretched. Events that in reality might take two seconds may take seven seconds. Through a series of tense close-ups, the moment is explored in depth.

Thus film, through the work of the editor, creates its own kind of time. Less freely than the printed page, more freely than theater, film can use time like putty.

OPTICALS. Before long, hundreds of shots have been spliced together like paragraphs in a book.

At major story divisions there may have to be a *fade-out* and a *fade-in*. These are like breaks between chapters. If they come at moments of heightened interest, they can whet the appetite.

Sometimes the *fade-out* and *fade-in* must overlap, forming a *dissolve*. This method may be chosen to emphasize close relationship between the overlapping events. The relationship may be one of causation, contemporaneity, similarity, or contrast.

Some film makers have a fondness for *matched dissolves*. Thus we have a fading glimpse of a young bridegroom saying "I do." An overlapping fade-in brings us, in the same position, the same young man in Army uniform, snapping to attention for the sergeant.

Dissolves and other *optical* effects, such as *superimposed* titles, are delegated by the editor to special technicians.

When the editing process has fixed the approximate length of the film and its portions, the center of attention can shift to the background music. This may be composed and recorded especially for the film, or in a low-budget film may be selected from *library music*, available on film or tape. Similarly, additional sound effects—trains, crickets, street sounds, surf—may be obtained from a sound-effects library on film or tape.

Then comes the crucial *mixing session,* when speech, sound effects and music are combined onto one tape. This is somewhat like the conducting of a symphony. First one element, then another, must take the aural spotlight. Finally the combined sounds are transferred from tape to film and combined with picture to make the composite film.

Every step of the way has involved different specialists. Every step, in live-action production, is expensive and complex.

But not more so than animation.

ANIMATION. Animation involves a wholly separate world of specialists.

In animation as in live action, 1440 pictures are shown every minute. In the fully animated cartoon, each of these 1440 pictures or *frames* may represent a different drawing, or several drawings.

In animation the sound track, instead of being finished last, may be attacked first. At least there must be early work on that element of the sound track that will control the timing of the action. This may be speech, music, or sound effects. When it has been recorded, the *exposure sheets* can be prepared.

The exposure sheets list all essential information about every frame, every twenty-fourth of a second, of the proposed film. They indicate the timing of each syllable, sneeze, breath or musical note, along with the action to accompany it.

Meanwhile the pictures work their way through another studio hierarchy. In close consultation with producer and director, a *designer* makes sketches showing the characters and general style of the film. When approved, these are arranged on the wall as a *story board,* following script chronology.

Based on story board and script, *animators* make careful

pencil drawings on paper of all key situations. Intermediate pencil drawings, also on paper, are made by assistant animators or *in-betweeners*.

Some drawings may be tested by being photographed and projected on a screen. If satisfactory, they go to *inkers,* who then trace the thousands of pencil drawings in special ink on celluloid sheets or *cels.* These are generally 8" by 12".

Special equipment helps the artists keep all drawings correctly positioned, and in perfect relationship to one another.

When the figures have been inked, they must be made opaque so that backgrounds will not show through them. So the inked cels go to painters or *opaquers.* This somewhat lower echelon of artist works on the reverse side of the cel, so that opaquing will not interfere with the inked outlines.

Finally the thousands of cels, with the instructions of the exposure sheets, go to the cameraman to be photographed on an *animation stand,* on which a camera is mounted face down. It can move up or down or rotate in any direction.

Beneath the camera are sliding parts on which cels can be fixed in layers. They can be moved in various directions, in minutely computed paths.

The animation camera is usually not set in automatic motion like the camera in a live-action production. Instead, each frame is taken separately. After each frame there may be a change of cels or adjustment in the positions of cels.

In the scene of the car bouncing crazily on the bumpy road, the bottom picture is the scenic background. After each frame, it is moved a fraction of an inch westward. The cel above it is the car. It too is moved a fraction of an inch after each frame, but in a jagged, hopping route that has been exactly plotted and is indicated on the exposure sheets. The third layer has the head and shoulders of the driver. After each frame, the cel on this layer is removed and a new cel

substituted, because this man is going through a change of
expression. The entire change of expression, lasting slightly
over two seconds, will involve fifty-eight different cels. On the
fourth or top level, another fifty-eight cels are used for the

PROD. NO.	CLIENT		PICTURE NAME	NO.	SCENE	FOOTAGE	SHEET NO.
112			"Suburbia"		6	92'	67

SYNOPSIS: Man chases train
ANIMATOR: CLF
ASSISTANT: PN
ANIMATION STAND NO. 1
START 4 FIELD

TRACK	ACTION	DIAL	BKGD.	TRAIN 1	WHEELS 2	BODY OF MAN 3	ARMS+ LEGS 4	DIAL		
WHISTLE:	TRAIN PULLS AWAY FROM STATION	1	#3		W-1		L-1	1	PAN	TRUCK
		2	RAILROAD	T-1	2	M-1		2	BACKGROUND	CAMERA
		3	STATION		3		2	3	RIGHT	BACK
		4			4			4	1/4 IN.	FROM
		5			1		3	5	PER	4 FIELD
		6			2			6	FRAME	TO
		7			3		4	7		11 FIELD
		8			4			8		IN
		9			1		5	9		48 FRAMES
		0			2			0		
		1			3		6	1		
		2			4			2		
		3			1		7	3		
		4			2			4		
		5			3		8	5		
		6			4			6		
		7			1		1	7		
		8			2			8		
MAN: W-1		9			3		2	9		
		0			4			0		
		1			1		3	1		
		2			2			2		
		3			3		4	3		
		4			4			4		
		5			1		5	5		
		6			2			6		
		7			3		6	7		
		8			4			8		
		9			1		7	9		
		0			2			0		
		1			3		8	1		
		2			4			2		
A	MAN FOLLOWS	3			1		1	3		
A		4			2			4		
A		5			3		2	5		
A		6			4			6		
A		7			1		3	7		
A		8			2			8		
A		9			3		4	9		
A - I -TT!		0			4			0		
		1			1		5	1		
		2			2			2		
		3			3		6	3		
		4			4			4		
		5			1		7	5		
		6			2			6		
		7			3		8	7		
		8		↓	↓	4	↓	8	↓	↓

man in the back of the car. This man has for efficiency been kept on an entirely separate set of cels, perhaps made by a different set of inkers and opaquers.

It will be seen why *cel animation* costs, at the least, thousands of dollars per minute.

Certain economies are possible. One economy is accomplished by reducing action to cycles.

ANIMATION EXPOSURE SHEET. Each horizontal line lists essential information on one *frame* of the proposed film: sounds, picture material, camera instructions. Sound is broken down, frame by frame, so that action can be synchronized to it. In the sequence here described, picture material for each frame will include background (railroad station) plus four cels, to be stacked as listed. For the body of the train one cel (T-1) will be used throughout the action. But the wheel motion is to be represented by a cycle of four cels (W-1, W-2, W-3, W-4), to be repeated a number of times. For the body of the man one cel (M-1) will be used throughout the action. But his arm and leg motions will be handled through a cycle of eight cels (L-1, L-2, L-3, L-4, L-5, L-6, L-7, L-8). The columns at the right indicate changes in the position of any of this material or of the camera in relation to it. On the first frame, only a small section of the stack of cels will be in the camera field. What the camera will photograph at this point is a 4-field—a field four inches wide. Camera will be moved back frame by frame so that eventually an 11-field, almost the whole 12-inch cel area, will be revealed. Information on 48 frames, or two seconds of film, is shown in this segment of an exposure sheet. The sheet has a double line after each 16 frames because this represents a foot of 35 mm film. A typical exposure sheet includes eighty frames. A ten-minute film would require 180 such sheets.

The movement of a child on a pogo stick can be depicted, let us say, in twelve drawings. This twelve-cycle movement might be repeated six times, while the background moves gently along. Three seconds of action would thus be accomplished by means of only thirteen drawings: the cycle of twelve plus a background. For complete animation, seventy-three drawings would be needed.

Economy thus encourages stylization. In animated cartoons we see horses running, girls dancing, people brushing their teeth, in cycles.

Some economies may be accomplished through use of puppets, hinged paper figures and similar devices. After each picture there is a minute change of position. Amount of artwork is reduced but camera time is not reduced.

On the whole, animation means large expense. Yet it is a constantly growing industry, important in entertainment, promotion, education, propaganda. It has made itself felt in political campaigns, labor relations, religion. What are the secrets of its strength?

Even at its lowest level, it has unique advantages. Precisely because it often deals with bizarre, unreal creatures, almost seeming to rule out identification, the animated film can appeal blatantly to hidden obsessions.

We have seen that animated figures can be, without moral censure, flamboyantly lawless. They are also omnipotent, exempt from all limitations of the physical world. They are secure: trap doors open for them but these creatures are indestructible. They go their unfrustrated way and nothing can stop them. Beneath the affable disguises, emotional identification is powerfully at work.

But the animated film also works at higher levels, and is winning the interest of leading artists everywhere.

SPECIAL-AUDIENCE FILM TECHNIQUES. We have mentioned that film, unlike press, began as a huge-audience medium, then learned to serve special audiences. It is important to consider some of the film's special-audience techniques.

Since economy is important in dealing with special audiences, we shall list the methods in order of cost progression. We start with those of lowest cost.

(1) *Filmstrip: silent.* The filmstrip, sometimes known as *slide film,* is a series of still pictures on a strip of 35 mm film. On the screen it appears identical to a series of slides. The filmstrip is projected on a special *filmstrip projector.*

The silent filmstrip is advanced, one frame at a time, by the push of a button. Each picture can be shown as long or as briefly as may be desired.

Filmstrips are widely used for education, training, orientation—in school, church, business and the armed forces. While used to some extent on television, their chief use is with groups, in situations supervised by a teacher or discussion leader. They are intended to serve as a teaching or discussion aid. Most filmstrips are silent, leaving commentary to the teacher or discussion leader.

An average silent filmstrip includes twenty-five to seventy-five pictures. Since each picture occupies only one frame, very little film is involved.

The filmstrip has to some extent replaced separate slides as lecture and classroom material. But not entirely. The lecturer using separate slides can rearrange them at will or sometimes skip a few. The filmstrip, while more convenient, involves a fixed progression. A degree of freedom has been sacrificed. A price has been paid for the added convenience.

(2) *Filmstrip: with sound.* As a further convenience, a disc recording is sometimes supplied with the filmstrip. It is

generally not more than fifteen minutes long, and is played on a record player.

Such recordings may include audible signals, to indicate points at which the filmstrip should be advanced to the next frame. Or there can be an inaudible signal which automatically advances the projector.

The sound filmstrip, in adding the convenience of sound, has also furthered rigidity. The tempo of the showing is no longer flexible. The filmstrip must now be shown at the speed dictated by the record, regardless of the audience's state of preparation. The role of teacher or discussion leader has been further reduced.

While the sound filmstrip quickly established its value, it proved troublesome in its need for both projector and record player.

The Navy had its own reason for being disturbed over this. After successfully testing sound filmstrips on land before World War II, it wished to extend their use to sea. But rolling seas made disc recordings unusable.

The Navy therefore transferred many of its sound filmstrips to 16-mm sound motion-picture film, to be projected on a normal 16-mm sound-film projector at twenty-four frames per second.

The product remained a filmstrip in effect, but had technically become a motion picture. The sound had become a normal sound track at the edge of the film. Each picture had become a series of identical frames. To be held ten seconds, a picture would be represented on the film by 240 identical frames.

Since all this increased costs without improving the final effect, the question arose, why not go further?

(3) *Camera animation.* The result is a kind of motion picture which the Navy has called a *filmograph.* Others have

called it an *animated filmstrip*. It includes techniques often referred to as *camera animation*.

The first purpose is to introduce, into the filmstrip effect, the element of movement. Instead of showing a still picture at equal distance for a full ten seconds, a dollying movement may be introduced. The camera starts on a detail, then pulls back. Or it starts on the full picture and moves in toward a significant detail. Either movement can be an exciting unfolding of details not seen at first glance. Sometimes the camera pans across a picture. Or a combination of several simultaneous movements is used.

Sometimes a single picture may yield several shots. George Stoney, directing *The Invader*, made a whole dramatic sequence out of one old photograph of 1890, showing the famous physician, Sir William Osler, at a hospital bedside with a group of medical students. First the full shot: the great teacher explaining the case. Then a close-up of his sensitive face. Then reaction shots of listeners. Then the ill man, looking up at the physician. Then the physician again. In such a sequence, some of the shots can involve movement.

The photography of still pictures with movement can be done with or without an animation stand. If an animation stand is used or its essentials devised, additional effects become easy without resort to expensive cel animation.

In showing on a map the deploying of forces at a famous battle, appropriate symbols can *pop on* as mentioned. The symbols can be made to move across the map, tracing battle routes.

Arrows can appear, to indicate direction of attack. Imaginative use of such devices is made in the Encyclopaedia Britannica film *The American Revolution*.

The *scratch-off* technique can likewise be used to show the development of a situation. In this method, for reasons that will presently be clear, the sequence is prepared in reverse.

Let us assume we are to see, on a map, the route traveled by an army unit during a campaign. The complete route is traced on glass or celluloid with crayon or paint that is easily removable. The glass or cel is placed over the map and the final situation photographed. Now a tiny fraction of the battle line is wiped or scratched off. The situation is again photographed. Then another fraction of the line is removed. The situation is again photographed. The process continues until the entire line has been removed. When run in reverse, the film will show the travels chronologically.

The sequence is photographed backwards because segments of line can more easily be removed neatly than added neatly.

In the photographing of a still picture, *overlays* are sometimes used to create what looks like a lighting effect. Such an overlay is simply a cel that has been shaded, except where the effect of concentrated light is needed. The overlay, as the name implies, is placed over the still picture.

Camera animation can further amend the filmstrip effect with occasional *dissolves* from still to still. This is done *in the camera* by turning the film back to an earlier position and making a second series of exposures. One series is made progressively weaker, the other progressively stronger.

The film *Challenge: Science Against Cancer* shows what can be done with this effect when combined with camera motion. A camera animation sequence gives the audience the sensation of moving through greatly magnified body cells, as if through inter-stellar space. Each shot is a still, photographed with dollying-in movement. A long series of such moving shots is overlapped, so that we seem constantly to move on toward new, mysterious galaxies.

These simple techniques can be used with great resourcefulness. Films for medical training use extensive camera animation. It is used in many commercials.

History and art films for education make increasing use of historic woodcuts, engravings and paintings, exploring them with carefully plotted camera movement, dissolves, overlays.

CAMERA ANIMATION was used in this sequence from *Home Homicide*, cartoon film directed by Abe Liss. The roller skate in one of the story board sketches was eliminated from the final plan. The action was accomplished by means of only: (1) littered stairway; (2) cut-out of the man. For each frame, the cut-out was simply moved south-southwest a fraction of an inch; it sailed in and out of sight in 26 frames. The simplified movements connected with this method—eliminating leg, arm, lip and other movements possible with cel animation—give the camera-animated film a style of its own, with its own charms and limitations. Sketches from story board by Paul Harvey.

A number of prominent modern artists have done paintings and drawings especially to be filmed with camera animation. The film *Hook*, drawn by Hazard Durfee, offers a fine example.

(4) *Painting on film*. A few animators have made a

specialty of painting directly on film, eliminating camera work. This highly specialized technique has yielded some interesting results.

(5) *Use of library footage*. What woodcut, engraving and oil painting were to former centuries, motion-picture footage is to our century. Billions of feet of film in the vaults of hundreds of companies tell the story of our century more vividly than could have been suspected by those who shot it. Entertainment features of yesterday are no less revealing than its newsreels.

Occasionally special needs send searchers back into those vaults. The anniversary of a state, manufacturing firm, university, political party or other association prompts a look at the past.

Organizations including government agencies, newsreel companies, film producers, business firms and international agencies maintain footage collections. They may make footage available by various arrangements. There may be a royalty payment of a few dollars per foot. Such charges, if made, vary according to intended use. The charge is higher for theatrical use than for educational use. It is higher for feature films than for short films.

Whether or not there is a royalty, the user generally pays the laboratory costs of duplication.

Combined with music and narration, library footage is a rich resource for special-interest films and occasionally for feature films. Such impressive projects as *The Pale Horseman* and *Victory at Sea* were based on historic motion-picture footage.

(6) *Actuality documentary*. Robert Flaherty, with films like *Nanook of the North* and *Man of Aran*, had a permanently unsettling effect on directors. The films were acted, but not by actors. To many directors, the acting of actors

16. STOCK
Troops move from stake to stake and are tested by multiple choice answers to given situation.

And you can always figure on the army for a new angle...This is called a stake course...you move from stake to stake and are tested on your knowledge of what to do in a certain situation...like map reading...You place a ring over the peg that represents the answer you think is correct. Simple, eh?...Well, maybe...

17. STOCK
Map reading check point. Soldier makes selection of answer on peg board.
(Hesitation before he does so.)

(SEQUENCES 14-17. Stake Training, LC 28843)

18. STOCK
Chemical battalion puts on a good demonstration on how to make a smoke screen.

(ESPC 82-52, 100 ft.)

Something a little tougher...a demonstration by a chemical battalion of how they work their "black magic" with smoke to save lives on the battlefield... Gee...my home chemistry set in the basement was nothin' like this

19. STOCK
House-to-house fighting in ruined city.

(LC 2764)

Storming an actual ruined town is a post-graduate course...the ruins are years old...the training is up to the minute.

20. STOCK
8" self-propelled howitzers moving down the road, then into position.

The sights you see in the army... all part of the training program, and sometimes better than the scenery.

LIBRARY FOOTAGE FILM. "Stock" footage collections of the armed forces provide almost limitless material for training and public relations films. Above, excerpt from *We Never Stop,* an Army report to the public on training methods.

would never again be a satisfactory medium for films of current history.

Many films have used nonactors for reasons of economy. People appearing as themselves are generally not paid, although they may be reimbursed for expenses.

However, the expected economies are often an illusion. Production with the nonactor cannot be done on rigid schedules. Hours may be spent on discussions, while costly technical crews stand waiting.

While there may be economies, they are not the best reason for using nonactors. Nothing can approach the truth of the nonactor, under the right kind of direction. A film like *The Quiet One* or *Still Going Places* is not achieved by handing a script to the nonactor. The dialogue must generally emerge from him—from his complete belief in the situation. Any falseness in a situation may freeze the nonactor so that he becomes incapable of going on. He may not even be aware of what is wrong. Then patient discussion is needed, and an entire scene may have to be reconceived. If this leads to more perfect truth, the director feels rewarded, with or without economies.

(7) *Sound film, shot silent.* There is one more cost-saving method. Many sound films, using actors or nonactors, are shot silent. Sound elements are added later, and may include narration, music, sound effects or a combination of them.

Occasionally dialogue is so added. It may be *post-synchronized,* as in *The Bicycle Thief* and many other Italian films. That is, lines of dialogue are later fitted to silently filmed action. In such films the dialogue is often used with long shots or medium shots, to conceal synchronization problems. In close-up passages, there is likely to be much use of reaction shots.

Silent shooting is more economical than sound shooting,

but post-synchronization is time consuming and will reduce the savings.

This concludes our listing of less-expensive film techniques. Most can hardly be called "inexpensive." The next step up in the price scale brings us back to synchronized sound shooting with professional performers, with all the complexities of cost involved.

PURPOSE: DISCUSSION. We have seen that larger budgets have brought us, at each point, new advantages. But for each advantage something was lost. On the way up, for example, the discussion leader was lost.

It will be recalled that slides and filmstrips gave him a dominating role. They were tools for his use.

Gradually, the fast-growing film pushed him aside.

This is no trivial problem. When a film succeeds in channeling inner drives toward new ideas and actions, it is seldom through its own impact alone. It succeeds, in the end, through the face-to-face relationships it sets in motion.

This suggests the importance of those films which are planned not as a finale, but as an overture to face-to-face communication. Focusing deep drives toward new ideas, they hand the spotlight to the audience and its discussion leader. In successful communication the audience must be no bystander, but the chief actor.

Controls: Film

TRAFFIC REGULATIONS. Like press, film is surrounded with an increasing number of traffic problems.

As with the press, these include the developing doctrine of the right of privacy. In films this means the right not to have one's likeness or voice used without consent for entertainment, promotion, propaganda. The documentary film producer must get written releases from all participants.

Other problems have to do with rights of authors, composers, publishers. Film brought new extensions of copyright legislation.

Other problems have to do with libel laws; with the rights of artists and technicians as embodied in union agreements; with patent rights.

CENSORSHIP. Film also has problems of censorship. Moves for censorship began early in motion-picture history, for reasons already discussed.

Were films a part of the press, entitled to that freedom guaranteed in the First Amendment? Some thought so.

But in 1915 the United States Supreme Court refused to set aside state censorship laws of Kansas, Ohio and Pennsylvania, expressing the view that movies were mere "spectacles." Official censorship thus became a fixture in these states and later in Maryland, New York, Virginia. It also became established in many cities.

Official film censorship in the United States reached its high-water mark in the 1920's and the 1930's. It then began a decline, for which there are several reasons.

One is the rise of 16 mm films. State censorship laws forbid the showing of films in public without prior approval of censors. But showings in schools, clubs and churches have not been considered *public* showings. This has reduced the effectiveness of censorship rulings and sometimes made them seem absurd. Thus *Feeling All Right,* a film on venereal disease, was banned by the New York State censors as obscene. Meanwhile it was distributed within the state by official health and education agencies—to schools, colleges, churches. City College of New York gave the film an award.

Another factor in the decline of censorship was the rise of television. With the coming of television, the Pennsylvania board of censors notified television stations in the state that films must be approved by the board before being telecast. Television stations contested this and won a court decision. This made it possible for television to show films banned from theaters.

Supreme Court decisions of the 1950's suggested that the Court had changed its view of 1915. In 1953, the Court overruled New York State's banning of *The Miracle,* finding certain clauses in the state censorship law too vague to be valid. The Ohio censorship law was then undermined by an Appellate Court decision. These developments placed stricter limits on the areas in which official censorship might operate.

All this centered the spotlight on other kinds of restraint.

INDUSTRY CENSORSHIP. The major film producers, trying to ward off official censorship and other interference, established the Hays Office in 1922 and in 1930 strengthened it with a production code. A Production Code Administration was later set up and given power. The major producers bound themselves not to issue films without a seal of approval from the Code Administration. Appeal procedures were provided. Fines of twenty-five thousand dollars could be imposed for violations of the system.

This was the most elaborate self-censorship system devised by any mass medium. It has been ardently supported and as vigorously attacked. Like official censorship, it has declined in power—for several reasons.

When the system was first established, the major producers owned or controlled most theaters. But a federal antitrust action, *The United States v. Paramount,* "divorced" exhibition from production and distribution. One result was that it became possible for independent producers to get films shown without the seal of approval. A number of films, such as *The Moon Is Blue* and *The Man With the Golden Arm,* have been distributed without the seal. Wide acceptance of such films has weakened the prestige of the Code.

Television also weakened the Code. For example, in 1955 the Production Code Administration, bound by its rules against kidnaping stories, refused to approve *Ransom!* when the script was first submitted by Metro-Goldwyn-Mayer under the title *Fearful Decision*. The producer appealed, pointing out that the story had twice been telecast coast-to-coast by the Theatre Guild under sponsorship of United States Steel, winning favorable mail and press comment and no protests. The Production Code Administration then changed its decision, on the technical ground that the kidnaping itself was not shown.

All this suggests the difficulty of embodying, in a set of rules, the moral values of communication.

The censor's impulse is to combat evil by tipping the scales against it in story and drama. He says to the producer: "Don't let Cain kill Abel—just have him hurt him a little." Or: "Don't let Eve eat the apple—at least let her do it off screen."

This may be a normal, ethical impulse. But it may also misinterpret the role of communication. Banning evil example from film does not ban it from life. It may not strengthen our power to cope with it. It may have the opposite effect.

Code rules multiply, but they do not produce morality. They do not stop vulgarity. Trying to banish forbidden impulses, censors may only change the disguises in which they appear. They ban passionate love-making, and excessive violence takes its place.

OTHER RESTRAINTS. Besides the waning restraints of official censorship and industry censorship, there is the restraining influence of citizen groups. Some publish ratings, classifying films according to suitability for different groups. Among

these is the Legion of Decency, whose members take a pledge
not to attend condemned films.

But perhaps the strongest pressures on the producer are
those which stem from the growth of his industry. The very
complexity of the industry is a conservative force. To make
this clear, let us examine the industrial transition of the
film world.

The Great Transition: Film

First came small producing units of three or four people,
making a film in a day. They would sell prints directly to
exhibitors. The exhibitors, besides running these films, presently ran advertising slides for local merchants. The total
situation:

An exhibitor, having run a film a few dozen times, could
use it no more. He might try to trade with other exhibitors.
But his stock of old, useless films kept growing. They were
a fire hazard and an exasperation. Many were thrown
away.

Into this wasteful system stepped a new figure. A middleman began to buy prints from producers, then *rent* them for
short periods to exhibitors. The middleman's storage depot
became known as an *exchange,* since it seemed an extension
of the trading system.

EXCHANGE. The new system was obviously a blessing to

all concerned. The producer no longer had to deal with hundreds of exhibitors. The exhibitor no longer had to store unwanted films. Henceforth exhibitors would turn to exchanges for a steady supply of films on a rental basis.

Thus distribution became a major factor in motion pictures along with production and exhibition. Some distributors became regional distributors with one or two exchanges; others, national distributors with perhaps thirty exchanges.

Soon production, distribution and exhibition were joined by a fourth major element—investment capital:

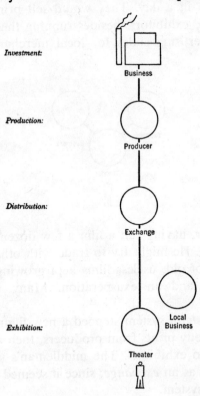

Investment:

Business

Production:

Producer

Distribution:

Exchange

Exhibition:

Local Business

Theater

Demands for expansion, for multi-million-dollar features, for reorganizations needed after new inventions—such as sound, color, wide screen—made producers more and more dependent on investors. These, investing in films as a business, acquired a major voice in policies.

Now those in investment, production, distribution and exhibition acquired a life-and-death dependence on each other.

Meanwhile two powerful trends, directly opposed to each other, were at work. We saw these same trends in the newspaper field.

One was toward fragmentation. As each new special skill developed, it became the basis for new, independent companies. New firms sprang up around such technical services as: laboratory work, stock footage, sound effects footage, music footage, animation services, puppetry, newsreel services, title art, photomicrography, equipment rental, studio rental.

The other trend was toward consolidation, by purchase or merger—to protect sources and markets, diversify investments, effect economies, meet opposition.

In exhibition this resulted in chains of hundreds of theaters. Joining all levels, the trend resulted in huge production-distribution-exhibition combinations.

Thus Metro-Goldwyn-Mayer and related companies have owned *theaters;* maintained distribution *exchanges,* serving their own theaters as well as others; acted as *producers;* maintained supporting studios, laboratories and other *technical services;* maintained *newsreel* staffs and related services; and operated such *other services* as footage library, animation facilities. Functions performed by MGM are shaded in the following chart.

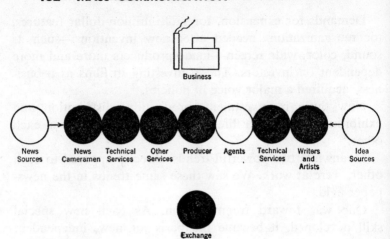

Business

News Sources | News Cameramen | Technical Services | Other Services | Producer | Agents | Technical Services | Writers and Artists | Idea Sources

Exchange

Local Business

Theater

In addition Metro-Goldwyn-Mayer has moved into such adjacent fields as music publishing (Robbins Music, Inc., Miller Music Corporation, Leo Feist, Inc.); radio station operation (WMGM, New York); program syndication (MGM Radio Attractions); phonograph records (MGM Records).

In film as in press, the trend toward combinations has at times seemed overwhelming. But in film as in press, other factors counteracted the trend.

We have mentioned the federal antitrust action that forced the separation of exhibition from production and distribution.

Since then the producer, no longer controlling his first outlet, has increasingly sought security in new outlets: television, school, church, business firm. These involve him increasingly with a special kind of investor—the sponsor:

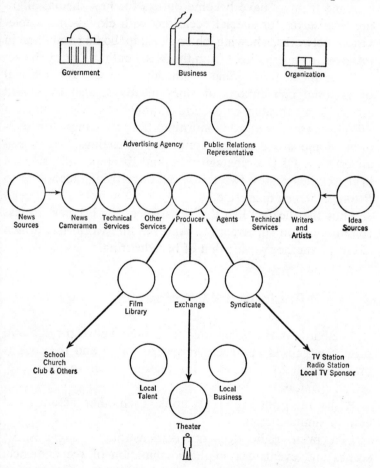

Meanwhile exhibitors, no longer controlled by producers, became retailers with some bargaining powers. As among newspapers, this did not necessarily result in great local initiative. Yet the outlet now had choices.

Some have begun to show a steadier trickle of foreign films.

Some theaters have become outlets for new media, aligning themselves for special occasions with closed-circuit television networks, showing championship boxing matches in progress, or opera direct from the Metropolitan Opera House.

Some theaters are joined with other theaters for national or regional conventions or sales meetings, also by closed circuit. Some theaters emphasize community services, housing PTA-sponsored Saturday-morning film showings for children. Some are used for community meetings. Many sell advertising. Of the nineteen thousand theaters and drive-ins in the United States, two thirds sell advertising, according to *Business Screen* magazine.

Thus the theater, like the newspaper, has become a mass communication supermarket. And the film world has drawn closer to another world: that of broadcasting.

3 Radio and Recordings

The battle in the home was, for a time, between radio and print. Unfocused audiences seized on radio and the sounds of life. Focused audiences, for reasons we have seen, preferred print.

Radio and print, seemingly unlike each other, actually had certain similarities.

Like print, radio does not demonstrate. It suggests. Its scenes and events are in the imagination of the audience. Because of this, radio is almost as mobile as print. It need not wait for scene carpenters or camera crews. Impossible settings are easy.

Like print, radio does not *require* a setting. Film is sometimes hampered by the difficulty of getting away from the idea of setting. In radio as in print, a narrator has freedom: he may speak from a specific time and place, or from no time and no place.

In radio as in print, narrators are easily accepted.

Essentially, radio is a narration medium. At first it was all narration, at least in form. Announcers kept telling things: the totals for Harding, the score of the game, the news of the hour, the name of the musical number.

But with all this, one added factor made radio's narration different from printed narration: the sounds of people and things. Voice, sound, music touched hidden impulses, started identifications, took people to distant, magic places like Pittsburgh or the Coconut Grove. This factor of sound, a dramatizing factor, drew millions to the loudspeaker.

As radio grew, it became dissatisfied with narrative forms. It wanted to be "show business." But with the coming of television, radio's limitations became clear. Radio could not be show business because it could not show. In a contest for attention, words could not win against pictures. As television captured the living room, radio took to the kitchen, bedroom, bathroom, basement, workroom, car.

Radio had to find a new niche for itself. It found it—in its own unique weakness.

WEAKNESS IS STRENGTH. Radio is the one medium that cannot seize the eye. It is therefore the one mass medium that can serve an active audience: getting up, bathing, eating, doing housework, shopping, commuting, picnicking, camping, cooking, going to bed.

Radio became a symbol of the competitive determination of the mass media to occupy any remaining fragment of audience attention. Radio's role became that of constant companion.

New, lighter radios favored this role. But it required different programming. One-hour dramas were no good on the way to the airport. Complex production effects couldn't compete with razor, pop-up toaster, or baby in the back seat. Simplicity became a keynote. So did economy. Millions were still listening but fewer at a time.

So radio once more concentrated on narration: disc jockey, commentary, newscast, sportscast, on-the-spot interview, lecture, reading, sermon. Dramas became fewer in number. Those that remained tended to be short and simply constructed. Often narration dominated.

This new emphasis on narration did not hurt radio. Radio thrives on simplicity. Like poem and cartoon, radio works best with economical means.

To its narration, radio can add dramatic impact with three elements: (1) sound effects, (2) music, (3) dialogue.

(1) *Sound effects.* Sounds make pictures. But unlike pictures on the printed page, a sound is always something happening. This is the dramatic secret of sound.

While the eye can perceive things at rest, the ear cannot. Therefore every sound says: "Action!"

The mind cannot always tell *what* action. It may need help from words. Some sounds identify themselves: *old railroad train, crickets, wind*. Others do not: *diesel train, rain, waterfall*. But with the right advance suggestion from words, any sound is compellingly real.

Because sounds act as an alert, signaling action, they are valuable dramatically. But like all alert signals, they must not be overused.

Sound effects are used in dialogue scenes and also as accompaniment to narration. In radio many children's stories have been narrated with the aid of this one dramatizing factor.

With expectations developed by words, a single sound effect can have the impact of dramatic vignette.

As in film, sound can be used selectively. A naturalistic mixture of night sounds may baffle and frustrate the mind. The single sound of *frogs* may set it to work. The aim is not completeness but audience activity.

(2) *Music.* In radio and recordings music can occupy the spotlight by itself. This is true of no other mass medium. Only here is music more than an accessory.

Music, like sound, is a kind of dramatization. It invites that suspension of self which we found to be the key to submerged emotion.

Like other means of drama, music touches deep obsessions. Like all drama, it deals in symbols that acquire full meaning only from what they may stir in the unconscious. "All music," said Walt Whitman, "is what awakens from you when you are reminded by the instruments."

In radio storytelling, music is used with narration more often than with dialogue. Used with narration, it adds a dramatic dimension to what is essentially nondramatic.

In popular song, the dramatic impact of music is combined with lyrics dealing with universal fantasy themes. Here the appeal is constantly to basic emotions: taboo obsessions, omnipotence obsessions, security obsessions.

It should be noticed that the appeal to such obsessions, as exemplified in the hit songs of any recent period, is almost as direct as that of the animated cartoon. Music, like the cartoon, provides a disarming disguise. It offers itself as ritual, social convention, a pattern for a dance. Yet beneath this surface it enlists the most compulsive identification. Radio's continuing hold on the unfocused audience rests in large part on this appeal.

The emotional leverage of words-and-music is exemplified by the radio's singing commercial. Few forms of advertising have aroused so much resentment; few have been so successful. In television the singing commercial has formed a natural alliance with the cartoon commercial.

To the extent that it is accepted, the singing commercial is taken up by the audience. The message is carried over into face-to-face communication. Thus, to the advertiser, music has a built-in merchandising factor.

The strong feelings aroused by singing commercials led to sociological studies. These seemed to show that the young prefer sung messages to spoken messages—a preference which recedes with age. Also, people of lower education prefer sung messages—a preference which recedes with higher educational levels.*

Such findings led to use of sung messages in public service promotion drives and propaganda drives aimed at lower socio-economic groups. In some cases these uses have met with considerable success. We shall consider this further in *The SPONSORS of mass communication.*

The singing of messages is, of course, founded on ancient tradition. What political movement, what religious crusade, has not had its theme song? What alma mater has not had its singing commercial, plugged by the faithful? For some, such messages are potent builders of devotion. Unlocked emotion flows readily into dedication.

For others, in whom the channel is blocked by resistance, the emotion becomes rising hostility. Power creates powerful boomerangs.

(3) *Dialogue.* In radio as in every medium, dialogue

* Lazarsfeld, Paul F.; and Kendall, Patricia L. *Radio Listening in America.*

readily involves its audience in human relationships. More easily than narration, it can encourage identification and awaken emotion.

But all-dialogue drama, standard in theater and film, is handicapped in radio. In radio drama of this sort, dialogue must constantly shed light on settings and props, and identify characters. For this reason radio has turned frequently to forms in which narration provides a framework, dialogue the emotional peaks. Such forms avoid radio's weakness while exploiting its mobility. Thus radio has used dramatized newscast, dramatized commercial, dramatized lecture, dramatized political argument, dramatized sermon.

In each of these, dialogue seems to excel in stirring emotion, narration in channeling it.

TAPE RECORDER. The advent of the tape recorder shifted attention to a new kind of dialogue: nonacted dialogue. By its reality, this instantaneously distinguishes itself from acted dialogue.

The magnetic tape recorder—first wire, then tape—made its American debut during World War II.* It was valuable in military intelligence. In addition, correspondents took recorders to battle fronts, recording their observations. They recorded descriptions while making parachute jumps. They interviewed men in action, at rest, in hospitals. The magnetic recorder made field-recording practical. It provided for the first time a recording system that was instantaneous, portable, accurate, and that permitted editing. From hours of material, minutes could be distilled for broadcast.

So compelling was the reality of this recorded material

* Magnetic recording originated in the nineteenth century. It was demonstrated by a Danish scientist, Valdemar Poulsen, in 1898. But like other communication inventions, it reached practical form long afterwards, under the stress of need.

"EMBEZZLER"

EXCERPT FROM TAPE #7:

HICKS: ...and you understand that no names will be used and
           no cities or identifications or anything of that
           kind that might identify you-- that's understood.

PATIENT: Yes, I understand that.

HICKS: If by any chance we do say anything here that-- uh--
           should be an identification, we'll just cut it out.

PATIENT: All right, I understand that.

HICKS: So-- anything you don't want said-- afterwards, if
           you'll just tell us--

PATIENT: All right. ***

HICKS: Then I'll just go ahead and we'll talk the thing out
           as far as we can.

(MUSIC: _DOWN UNDER_:)

TO BE RECORDED:

HICKS: This is George Hicks. The man who sat before me was
           guilty of embezzlement. From the company he worked
           for, a large corporation, he had stolen twenty thou-
           sand dollars in small amounts over many years. The
           embezzlement was skillfully done and it had taken the
           company a long time to find out what was happening.

           This man was well educated. At a prominent university
           he had earned a bachelor's degree, a master's degree,
           and an advanced engineering degree. The position he
           held with his company was important; he had been in
           charge of the whole Pacific Coast area. He was mar-
           ried and had one child. Now why did this man, so

that it quickly replaced actors on many kinds of programs: for example, on such current-history radio series as *The March of Time*.

Tape recorders have since been taken into prisons to record interviews with prisoners, yielding material for memorable radio documentaries on crime and the criminal. Commercials have featured man-in-the-street interviews and tape-recorded pickups from factories.

As in the film documentary, it is not customary to pay non-professionals appearing on documentary radio programs. This became an important economic factor.

In the new pattern of radio listening, intensive coverage is possible only through multiple broadcasts in each area. With acted drama, this means multiple fees to actors. Dramatization via field recordings avoids this skyrocketing cost.

Some of the savings are spent in editing. As in film, the spotlight shifts to the editing room. Sometimes hundreds of small segments are spliced together by the tape editor, working under supervision of the director. Digressions are omitted. New, stimulating juxtapositions are made.

By using three recorders, mixing is accomplished during

RADIO SCRIPT page, in standard radio form. Speaker's name is at side. Lower case letters are used only for speech. Directions are entirely in upper case. Music directions are, in addition, underlined. In this script, one portion is based on tape recording of announcer's interview with a patient—under treatment with a psychiatrist specializing in criminal cases. Asterisks *** indicate where tape editor is to eliminate material in original interview. Excerpt is from *Why Did He Do It?*, recorded mental health series produced by Center for Mass Communication at Columbia University, in consultation with David Abrahamsen, M. D.

the editing process. Music on one recorder, narration on another, are mixed onto a third with proper relative volumes. Sound effects are added. Parallel items are brought together in a montage threaded by music.

The tape recorder gave radio a new tool of dramatization. Here is the excitement of reality, but reality that can be stripped of formlessness and tooled with selectivity.

It offers the technical possibility of outrageous falsification. Since a small word like "not" can be eliminated, a man's voice can be made to say the opposite of what he meant and said. As in every medium, protective laws and precedents have developed. The concept of *invasion of privacy* grows with each new medium.

SIMPLICITY. We have seen that radio narration can, for emotional drive, call on three tools of dramatization: sound effects, music, dialogue. But often it does not need these tools. Circumstances surrounding narrator and broadcast may provide the drive.

A talk by the President from the White House, in a time of international tension, hardly needs motivation-building by sound effects, music or dialogue episodes. To the extent that such devices are unneeded, they are unwelcome.

The success of many public appeals has been due less to the devices used than to the affection and respect commanded by the speaker.

This puts the emphasis where it belongs in radio: on *simplicity*. Compared to the complexity of film and television, radio is simple. The mind does it.

This has given radio special appeal to various groups. To poets, for example. Archibald MacLeish wrote: ". . . the technique of radio, the ordinary, commercial technique, has developed tools which could not have been more perfectly adapted to the poet's uses had he devised them himself. . . .

The announcer is the most useful dramatic personage since the Greek chorus." *

Simplicity also means economy. This factor has made radio valuable to many organizations not able to afford film or television. It has also made it possible for some stations to perform specialized functions such as serving Negro audiences, foreign language groups, religious denominations, campus students.

Among the important special-interest stations are the educational stations run by boards of education in large cities. Their services include programs for classroom listening in schools and programs for adult education.

Controls: Radio

TRAFFIC REGULATIONS. Radio, like other media, is surrounded by increasing traffic regulations, dealing with libel, invasion of privacy, copyright, unfair competition, false advertising. In addition, there is a group of regulations new with radio, relating to the Federal Communications Commission.

For a time in the 1920's, chaos ruled the ether as each station chose its own spot on the dial. Exasperated broadcasters and public appealed to government for traffic direction. It was the first time, said Herbert Hoover, that business begged for government interference. Congress then set up the Federal Radio Commission, and later the Federal Communications Commission.

The FCC acts under legislation that has proved of crucial importance to mass communication.

The law is clear: no broadcasting station owns the frequency it uses. This belongs to the people. The station re-

* MacLeish, Archibald. *Fall of the City,* foreword. New York: Farrar & Rinehart, Inc. 1937.

ceives a license from the FCC, giving it the right to use the frequency for a limited period, usually three years. At the end of this period the station may apply for a renewal of its license. It is the right and duty of the FCC to consider this application in the light of the station's service to the "public interest, convenience and necessity."

The FCC has severely limited the number of stations that may be owned by one organization. This move closely parallels federal action in the film field, separating exhibition from production and distribution.

The station's public-service obligation includes equal treatment, during political campaigns, of candidates for the same office. Time of equal value must be available on the same terms to each, whether given or sold. The station must avoid certain categories of material, such as the profane and obscene.

But the law is equally clear on something else: the FCC may not censor. It has the right to review past performance, not to veto proposed programs.

Thus the law gave radio simultaneously two things: (1) responsibility to the public; (2) freedom from censorship.

These same elements, taken into television, have tended to influence all mass communication. With all media increasingly involved in the affairs of others, all become increasingly involved in the public responsibilities of broadcasting. And the broadcaster's freedom from censorship undermines all organized censorship. Instead we find the emphasis shifting to *definition of responsibility*.

But if broadcasting is free from official censorship, it is not free from restraints. We mean, once more, the restraints that come from industrial organization.

Let us review the organization of radio. It is particularly important to us because it provides the starting framework for television.

The Great Transition: Radio

At first there was only the broadcaster, aided by local volunteer talent and, presently, local advertisers:

Everything was local. To large advertisers the arrangement was neither attractive nor convenient. Presently a plan was proposed to help stations serve large-scale national advertisers.

NETWORK. An organization was set up in New York. From the American Telephone and Telegraph Company it leased special long-distance lines on an annual basis. To this New York organization, several dozen stations gave an option on specific periods of their time.

Now the organization, calling itself a *network*, was in a position to sell to advertisers identical time on several dozen stations, all in one transaction. The revenue from such sales was divided between station and network, with the network keeping the larger share.

Presently the network was adding other services for this larger share. Over the leased wires it provided the station with programs to fill unsold periods. These came to include news and special-event programs from points far and near. They also came to include prestige programs such as symphony concerts.

With some oversimplification, this describes the plan behind the development of the National Broadcasting Company, formed in 1926, and the Columbia Broadcasting System, formed in 1927. The network idea does not require ownership of stations, although both these networks did buy stations in key cities. Basically, the network is a web of contracts, facilitating the sale of time to national sponsors and serving as distribution mechanism for programs of national interest.

ADVERTISING AGENCY IN RADIO. To win sponsors for such programs, the early networks had to win the interest of advertising agencies.

The first step was to offer advertising agencies an arrangement identical to that established by the printed media: a 15 per cent agency commission. If an agency, on behalf of a sponsor, contracts for a weekly period at six thousand per week, then the network bills the agency at six thousand dollars minus 15 per cent, or at the weekly rate of fifty-one hundred dollars. The agency bills the sponsor for the full six thousand, earning nine hundred dollars per week.

In placing the order through a particular agency, and helping it earn a nine-hundred-dollar weekly brokerage fee, the sponsor expects and receives certain services from the agency: selection and supervision of program, preparation of commercials and other services.

Choice of program may mean selection of a program already on the air, or the building of a new program. At first, when there was little well-known talent on the air, advertising agencies took the lead in building new programs. Drawing stars, writers and directors from theater and vaudeville, some agencies became huge program-producing organizations.

The agency's program expenditures have generally been billed to sponsors *plus* 15 per cent. This may mean another fee comparable to the time-brokerage fee. The large advertising agencies, strengthened by commissions on time and talent, quickly became powerful forces in network programming, often able to draw top executives away from networks.

In time this drift stopped. One reason was the rise of a new element: the independent producer.

PRODUCER. Of the hundreds of advertising agencies active in broadcast advertising, many were not able to build, overnight, program-producing divisions. The independent program producer developed to meet the needs of these agencies. The independent producer may be one man or a large organization.

The independent producer is not involved in advertising or time buying. He does not compete with the advertising agency for its time-brokerage fees. He seldom deals directly with sponsors. He merely offers to relieve the advertising agency of the problem of building and supervising a program.

He generally says to the agency: "My organization can produce for you this program, with these stars, by these writers, for a weekly lump sum of five thousand dollars per week." Occasionally a cost-plus-percentage arrangement is made. But the lump-sum arrangement is usual. Offering a five-thousand-dollar *package,* the producer has probably budgeted his costs at not more than four thousand dollars per week. Because of the lump-sum arrangement, the independent producer is often called a *package producer*.

At first some large advertising agencies were reluctant to do business with package producers, feeling that their own prestige required having a program-producing division. This prejudice gradually vanished. Many agencies became so large as to be unwieldy. They began to prefer doing business with independent producers, reserving to themselves a supervisory function. Buying a program as a package for five thousand dollars per week they would generally add a commission for their own supervision, billing the sponsor at $5,750 per week.

Meanwhile to serve the needs of producers, many special technical services developed, as in the film field: sound effects, music, recording, contest management. Thus the assembly line became:

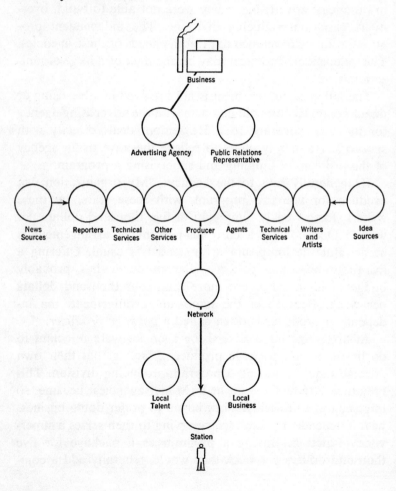

STATION. We must return now to the local station. We mentioned that in the sale of time to national sponsors, the station receives the smaller share of revenue. This has always irked the local station.

It accepted the arrangement because it offered at first the only road to prestige. It was the only way of getting programs from large entertainment centers, with famous talent, sponsored by national advertisers. All this yielded prestige, helped in securing local sponsors.

But the local sponsors were always, financially, more important to the station than the national sponsors. Selling a local half hour direct to a local department store for one hundred dollars, the station could keep the entire amount. Selling a similar period via network and advertising agency to a cigarette manufacturer, the station might net only thirty dollars.

Thus it was important to the station that the network agreement reserved certain periods as *station time,* earmarked for local business.

At first this local business was served almost entirely with local talent. This might be excellent but might lack glamour.

Local talent, like the local newspaper, can make a local appeal. But the local business may be more interested in developing a big-business aura.

Into this dilemma a new kind of organization injected itself: the program syndicate.

PROGRAM SYNDICATE. The syndicate produces a series of twenty-six, thirty-nine or fifty-two recorded programs, and offers these to the local station for local use. A series may have cost four thousand dollars per program to produce. It is made available to a local Rochester bakery, for use over a Rochester station, for seventy-five dollars per program. A

Cincinnati dairy sponsors it in Cincinnati for a hundred dollars per program. A Houston bank sponsors it in Houston for ninety-five dollars per program.

In some areas a regional sponsor may buy the series in several markets. Thus a Michigan brewer may buy the series for nine stations in Michigan for a weekly total of $760. Syndication fees are scaled to the size of the market or to station time rates. Each sponsor adds his own commercials. The programs are constructed so as to leave periods of time for local commercials. For this reason, these programs are often called *open-end programs*.

Sometimes local commercials are made in New York or Hollywood with the program star. Thus a star may record, in one hour, twenty-six commercials for a Tulsa restaurant.

Via film, the open-end program quickly became important in television.

PRESS ASSOCIATION IN BROADCASTING. Applying the same principle to news, stations can buy news from the press associations, as do newspapers. The news comes from AP, UP or INS over printer-telegraph machines. United Press was the first to launch a broadcasting service distinct from its newspaper service. The material for broadcasters is written for voice delivery; it includes one-minute flashes, five-minute summaries, fifteen-minute newscasts, scripts for sport broadcasts, farm broadcasts, women's broadcasts and other special purposes. Material can be torn off as received. It can be read from the original sheets or rewritten by the local station. It can be sponsored by local sponsors.

As in the newspaper field, syndication and press-association services have been criticized as causing standardization. Stations throughout the country broadcast the same syndicated news bulletins, commentaries and features.

But another effect should be mentioned.

In the early days of network broadcasting, syndication was not practical because of the poor recording quality. For local stations there was only one road to prestige programming: network affiliation. This made local stations very dependent on networks.

When the syndicated program rose to importance during the 1940's and 1950's, the balance shifted. Now local stations could serve local sponsors with Eddie Cantor, Humphrey Bogart, Tyrone Power.

In the 1930's, a listener could always tell a non-network station from a network station by its programming. Then the distinction began to blur.

Presently the program sponsored by a small local business might have the same big-enterprise air as the program of a giant corporation. Now the local station became more independent toward the network. The station's bargaining power increased. If syndication increased standardization, it also strengthened the independence of the local outlet.

In fact, syndication became so important to the station, that the networks began to serve their affiliates with a similar device. They began to broadcast network programs with gaps for commercials, to be inserted locally. In these *local-participation programs* the network wires serve as the mechanism of syndication. Thus the network began to serve local as well as network advertisers.

STATION REPRESENTATIVE. The local station, with varied program sources, can serve not only local sponsors but also national sponsors. Like the newspaper, the station maintains a representative in large cities to push the sale of time to advertising agencies for major clients. It can serve such sponsors via local live programs or syndicated programs.

Thus national advertising can reach the local station via two routes—in television as in radio:

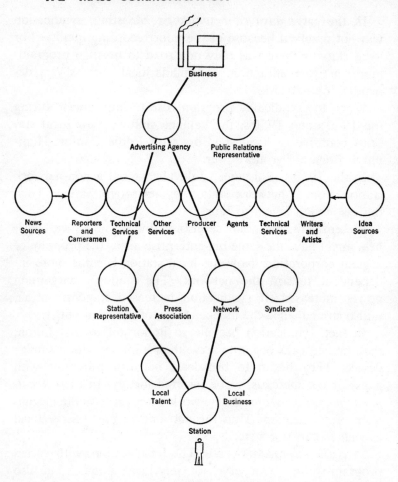

The station can also get big-name talent via two routes: network and syndicate. It also gets national news via two routes: network and press association.

It also gets free material—entertainment, news, promotion, education, propaganda—in script or recorded form from many organizations, including business, government agencies, citizen organizations:

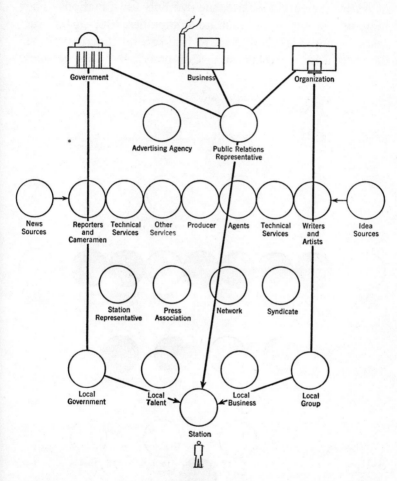

This makes the broadcasting station another mass communication supermarket. It can stock its shelves with many standardized items. It has room for local initiative, and in this lies its hope for individuality. Some seize this opportunity.

As in our earlier charts, the symbols are functions. They may be embodied in separate companies. But again, successful companies tend to move into several functions. In radio the National Broadcasting Company operates a *network;*

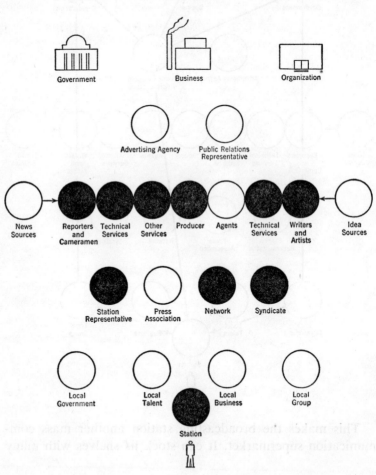

is a leading package *producer;* performs such *technical services* as recording and studio rental; *syndicates* programs; operates a few *stations;* and acts as national sales *representative* for its own stations as well as others.

In television the National Broadcasting Company developed corresponding operations. These have involved it inevitably in film: it is a film *producer,* a film *syndicate,* and operates a stock footage library.

Other companies illustrate other combinations of functions. Some advertising agencies are *also* public relations representatives and package producers. Some talent agents are *also* syndicates and producers—in various media. The integration of the media accelerates. The implications will be discussed presently.

4 Television

That television would turn out to be something quite different from radio-with-pictures was a foregone conclusion. That it would also be something different from movies-in-the-home may have been more surprising.

As soon as film men began to see films on television, they realized certain things. In films made for television they would have to rely more on close-ups, less on long shots. They would have to deal with smaller casts. They would have to forget about subtleties of lighting.

Almost immediately, theatrical film and television film began to part company. Theater film adopted the wide screen, emphasized spectacle, and asked writers for stories with seven or eight starring roles. Television emphasized intimacy, asking writers for stories with not more than three major characters.

A CBS television film producer, Irving Gitlin, said, "Television is a microscope, not a telescope."

LIVE TELEVISION. If filmed television immediately took new directions, it is not surprising that live television departed even more from screen habits.

There was every reason why this should be so. Filmed television was largely a Hollywood child; live television a New York child. Film habits continued to influence Hollywood; New York television was strongly influenced by men from theater and radio.

To many people, live television drama seemed to offer no advantage whatever over filmed drama. The producer of a live television drama would have to deal with the same elements as the producer of a film, but under circumstances that seemed at first glance almost hopeless.

Like the film producer, he would have to shoot a story from a variety of angles and distances. An audience habituated to constant shifts would not sit still for a static view. But live television, requiring continuous performance, would not allow the one-fragment-at-a-time procedure of film.

One lighting plan would have to do for a whole scene and all angles used in it. It would be a problem of lighting the set, not the shot.

Instead of one cameraman perfecting one angle at a time, three or four different cameramen would have to be in action simultaneously.

Instead of a director and editor evaluating the shots at leisure over a period of weeks, the editing would have to be done simultaneously with the shooting. Even while listening and watching, the director would have to "call out the shots" in the control room, signaling camera switches.

Meanwhile the actor, no longer concentrating on one shot at a time, would have to conceive and memorize his role as a whole, then play it out in a circle of light surrounded by constant activity: the slow, silent approach and departure of one dolly camera while a second pushes its nose through a window; the menacing descent, toward the bed, of a camera and cameraman on a boom; the constant overhead movement of microphones, shuttled and tilted.

What would come of it all?

The result was drama in which lighting was seldom subtle, in which actors sometimes fluffed and were seen to perspire, in which a microphone occasionally dipped into a scene. These were all sins that, in the *House Beautiful* atmosphere of many Hollywood films, would be inexcusable and contemptible. Why did people accept it? Why did they, by the millions, sit spellbound by live television? What was its appeal?

REAL TIME. It must be remembered that live television introduced something almost never seen in films: real time.

For decades the unit of production in motion pictures had been the shot. This was inevitable and right. We have noticed the flexibility and emotional power it gave the film. But something was lost as well as gained, although most people were never conscious of the loss.

By dealing with a few seconds at a time, the actor was seldom aware of his role as a whole. His main concern was, naturally enough, with the perfection of the moment.

The pace and rhythm of the play as a whole were partly a creation of the director, partly of the editor. We have seen that the latter could, in synthesizing hundreds of moments, depart far from actual time relationships. The result was the film's own kind of time, involving compression and expansion.

In the atmosphere of the motion-picture theater, the audience tends to be unaware of this. Where heads are vast and voices amplified, effects cannot be measured against reality. The value of factory-processed time relationships far outweighed any disadvantage.

But in television heads are close to life size. The distance between audience and show is a natural, person-to-person distance. Unrealities of timing and voice projection are felt. Effects are measured against reality. In this atmosphere the audience senses the reality of the real and the unreality of the unreal.

The pretelevision motion picture deified the actor while reducing his independence as an artist. He became necessarily one of the tools of the director.

Live television, like the theater, gives the actor central power. In the final broadcast the timing, the mood, the intensity of portrayal, are in his control. All this gives to many live television performances a type of unity difficult to achieve in motion pictures. It is an actor's unity.

But if the role of the actor has grown, that of director has certainly not been simplified. The complexity of technical elements which a director must co-ordinate during a live television production makes the motion picture seem an easy and restful medium.

TECHNICAL COMPLEXITY. In the network television drama there are generally three or four studio cameras. In the variety program there may be more. Occasional special programs have used dozens of cameras. In a short one-set program, such as a newscast, there may be two cameras or even one.

If the drama director has his way, one of his three or four cameras will be mounted on the type of dolly which the cameraman rides with the camera, so that he can shoot down on scenes from above, or swoop to positions close to the floor. Such an apparatus has to be pushed around by an assistant—in some cases by two assistants. Other cameras are moved around by the cameramen themselves.

In addition to the action in the studio, the program can use material from stills, film clips, slides. These generally come from a special room that may be far removed from the production studio. It generally has a variety of projectors: for 35-mm film; 16-mm film; opaque stills such as 4" by 5" *telop* cards; 2" by 2" slides; and sometimes other types of slides.

Each studio camera leads by cable to a monitor screen in the studio control room. Thus a row of screens, facing the director and his engineers and assistants, shows the images being picked up by the various cameras. Cameras and monitors have corresponding numbers: #1, #2, #3, #4. One monitor shows images from the film room.

A special monitor, often larger or set apart from the others, shows the picture in use at the moment. For a few seconds it may be the same picture as that on the #2 screen; then for a few seconds, the same as that on the #4 screen.

Another special monitor, the *preview monitor,* shows the picture about to be used, so that it can have a final check for content and quality.

The director or an assistant can talk at all times to the cameramen, so that the latter can through earphones get control-room comments and instructions.

Each camera is equipped with several lenses. The cameraman can revolve his lens turret to a new lens, and bring it into focus, in a second or two. He can also push his camera to another position, another set, in a matter of seconds.

In the *ad lib* program, such as a convention pickup, changes of position, angle, lens, may be decided on the spur of the moment and instructions relayed. In the drama program, all such matters are worked out in advance, so that spur-of-the-moment instructions may be restricted to re-finements.

The cameraman assigned to camera #2 in a broadcast of *Hedda Gabler* has before him, attached to his camera, a detailed schedule. It shows him that he has, during the broadcast, forty-seven different shots. He will begin his work in the bedroom by picking up Hedda Gabler as she rises from her dressing table, yawns, and moves toward the door. He pans with her to the door.

Then, when the light on his camera goes out, he knows he is no longer *on the air*. Hedda, moving through the hall, is being picked up by #1. Meanwhile #2 must move to his next position, in the garden. He has forty-two seconds to get there and be ready. Hedda Gabler has a brief conversation in the living room with her husband and his aunt. This is being covered by #3 and #4. Then she moves into the garden, followed by her husband. As they come outdoors, #2 is ready for them with his wide angle lens. Meanwhile #1 has moved into position near him for a close-up of Hedda. During this close-up #2 must change lenses for a close-up of the husband. Then follows a rapid alternation of close-ups of him and Hedda. During the third close-up of the husband, #2's instructions tell him he must be moving in to a *very tight close-up*. Then, as Hedda angrily returns to the house, the action once more centers in the living room and is mainly covered by #3 and #4. But #2, too, has a function in this scene. At one point, as Hedda approaches the large fireplace, #2 shoots her through the fireplace. The fireplace backing of black cloth is lifted by a stagehand for this four-second shot and is then restored to place. Then #2 wheels to the bedroom, later to the hallway, then to an easel used in the first commercial.

Routes, positions, lenses are all decided. Only the precise moments of the switches from #1 to #2 to #4 to #3 require off-the-cuff decision. The director, waiting for a particular smile, a particular look of terror, calls out the moment. A technician's touch of the button makes the switch.

STUDIO EXPENSES. It will be seen that studio rehearsals involve fabulous expense. A cameraman in action means a chain of control-room technicians in action. It means studio electricians and stagehands in action. Sound requires boom men, sound-effects operators, and control-room sound engineer in action. Rehearsal may require reservation of a line to the film room, and men on duty in the film room. Scenery, made from blueprints in special carpentry shops, must have been transported and set up in this studio. All personnel is union personnel. Unlike film and radio, television was born at a time when unions in related fields were strongly established. Thus unionization began promptly.

When the lights are turned on in the television studio for a large drama rehearsal, the sponsor is immediately spending hundreds of dollars per hour. In some cases, thousands. Therefore, everything must be done to reduce, through planning and preparation, the time of studio rehearsals.

Casts seldom come to the studio until a day or two before broadcast.

They begin a week or two before with dry-run rehearsals. In a barren rehearsal room, the set is marked on the floor, often laid out in broad stripes of black adhesive tape. These follow the scene blueprint to the inch. The scenery, designed weeks before, is meanwhile under construction elsewhere.

The director, directing his cast within the striped areas, knows exactly how each scene will be photographed. Sets, action, camera movement must all be planned in relation to one another, as well as in relation to other factors such as

"A SLIGHTLY IMPORTANT MAN"

ACT ONE	C.U. Ledger ①

✓Cue Fred

FADE IN:

A SMALL, RATHER DILAPIDATED OFFICE.
NIGHT. THERE IS A SINGLE WINDOW,
BEYOND WHICH WE SEE A FIRE ESCAPE.
THERE IS AN OLD-FASHIONED ROLL-TOP
DESK, WITH A WOODEN SWIVEL CHAIR. ON
THE WALLS ARE A GREAT MANY FRAMED
PICTURES OF THEATRICAL CELEBRITIES,
ALL OF THEM AUTOGRAPHED. FRED BARTON
~~SITS AT THE DESK~~ IN HIS SHIRT-SLEEVES,
WITH HIS NECKTIE PULLED DOWN, WORKING.
THERE IS A KNOCK AT THE DOOR. HE
DOESN'T EVEN BOTHER TO LOOK UP. ✓Cue

Dolly back
as Fred takes
ledger, goes
U.C. to adding
machine.

Fred x's down
into camera,
sits at desk.
Dolly in

Sound
1 Knock

FRED

Come in.

Waist Tony ③
(in door)

(TONY ENTERS, CARRYING A SHEAF OF PAPERS.)

Pan Tony
to desk

TONY

I've got tonight's box-office receipts,
Mr. Barton.

E.T.
1 Fade out

FRED

Put them here, Tony.

Let Fred
on

TONY *(pause)*

(sits)
(HOPEFULLY) Business was a little

better tonight. The house was about

three-quarters sold out.

Dolly in as
Tony sits

FRED
(reaches for pen)

(CONTINUING TO WORK) Good.
(works)

Dolly in tight
to Fred.
Lose Tony
C.U. Tony ②

TONY *(pause)*

And the advance sale for next week is

a lot better than I thought it would be.

available floor space, scene budgets, personnel. If a lady star's contract requires that close-ups be shot from the right side only, this will affect action planning and possibly scene design.

A key scene is sometimes photographed with shots from three or four sides. This may call for such devices as: a wall hanging or picture that is slid aside for ten seconds to allow a camera shot; a hinged wall section that opens for twelve seconds, then is back in place for a later reverse-angle shot; shots through windows, doors, fireplaces, stoves, closets.

Rehearsing, the director and his assistants sharpen their split-second plans. Late in the dry-run rehearsals, they may bring key technicians to watch—such as lighting director and audio director. These get their instructions, see a dry run-through.

Finally comes the time when cast, cameramen, sound engineers, control engineers, scene workers, electricians and assistants come together in the set, in the production studio.

TELEVISION SCRIPT is usually written in one narrow column, leaving remaining space for production notes. At some companies the left side, at others the right, is kept blank for this purpose. Above page shows how NBC director Edward King planned and directed the opening of a *Robert Montgomery Presents* program. Page suggests complexity of activity involved in even a simple sequence. This first page, representing 35 seconds of program time, used three shots, numbered by small numbers. These involved three different cameras, indicated by circled numbers. Camera movement was closely related to action. Director decided on some actor movements not called for in script. Music was via electrical transcription (ET), meaning recording. Script by Noel Gerson.

Now is the time when careful planning and rehearsals pay off, and lack of them brings catastrophe.

The director has under his supervision an agglomeration of artists and technicians. In a few hours he must make them into a team.

First the cast may do a run-through on the set, which they have never seen before—while cameramen and other technicians watch. Then cast and technicians go through the play together, with cameras, sound, lighting. Correcting errors, the director will for the moment ignore the total timing. In this stop-and-go rehearsal there will be final decisions on such matters as lenses, lights and positions for the microphone boom. Key positions for actors and cameras may be marked on the floor.

At length comes an uninterrupted run-through. Then conferences and the polishing of muddy passages. Finally a dress rehearsal, perhaps with sponsors in an adjacent booth. Then more conferences, checking, reviewing, confirming, cajoling.

Now is the time when a sponsor begins to worry about a line that has been in the script since it was first submitted months ago, but that somehow doesn't sound as he imagined it. It seems to have implications he had not foreseen. The sponsor jots down an alternative line on an envelope.

But if he brings the matter up, he may be surprised. The advertising agency man may not be as eager as usual to carry out his slightest whim. The network producer may shake his head. As for the director, he may be unexpectedly explosive.

The sponsor may learn that the troublesome line is a cue—several cues. It is in the first place an actor's cue. It may be a cue for a switch. Or a cue for a cameraman to move to a new position. And a warning cue for a sound effect. Yes, it can be changed, at the risk of chaos.

A parenthetical result of the high cost of television has been that many programs are sponsored by several sponsors rather than one. This tends to remove the sponsor from the scene of action. He does not *sponsor the program;* rather he *buys an insertion.* Strengthening the position of the producer, this could bring long-range benefit to the medium and the sponsor. Certainly it is welcome to the director. It will be seen that the direction of a live program requires a combination of sensitive artistry and nerveless generalship.

Is it all worth it? What is gained, when it works, is a continuous performance. This means compellingly real continuity, real rise and fall of emotion, real interaction of people living together in real time. When the play is right, the impact can be extraordinary.

This is one reason why the film world, in its productions for television, began to adopt live television methods.

TELEVISION FILM METHODS. Before television, the film world had little reason to experiment with continuous performance. The idea offered hazards without apparent advantage. For half a century the success of film had been built on the splintering of time. But in television, reality had new value.

The television film producer had another reason for becoming interested in continuous performance: economy. Television films had to be produced for such budgets as twenty-five thousand to thirty-five thousand dollars for a half-hour film. In broadcasting terms this was lavish. In terms of theatrical film, it was shoestring financing.

Yet if the television film was to compete with the live program for sponsor investments, it would have to be done on the basis of such budgets. It could only be done by reducing to a minimum the man-hours of technical services.

This meant, as in live television, thorough rehearsals of casts in dry-run sessions. Then performance, with three or more cameras in simultaneous action.

After such a production session, three or more different versions of the photographed action are available. From these the final program is edited.

Because of raw stock, editing and laboratory costs, the television film is inevitably more expensive than a live program, even with continuous performance methods. But there are compensating advantages. Errors can be corrected. Most important of all, the film can be reused, in proportion to its value. It can be reused on television or in other ways. In television it can have one or more network uses and can then be syndicated. It can be used abroad. Nontelevision uses can include use in theater, school, church, club, business.

The continuous-performance method holds special advantage for comedy programs. In the theater, the laughter of the audience is part of the impact of the show. Television, like radio, addresses small, isolated audience units. Comedy producers have generally felt that these isolated units need the contagion of large-group laughter. Hence the studio audience.

But when a film is produced in bits, audience reactions are impossible. This problem has been attacked in several ways. One is the use of *dubbed* laughter—always a quickly recognized fraud. Another solution is to run the completed film for a studio audience, record its reactions, and combine these with the original film before broadcasting. This solution is practical but complex. A third solution is the continuous performance, filmed by several cameras before a studio audience. This is valuable not only for comedy but also for other programs in which audience reactions may be important: lectures, sermons, political talks.

These are, in Plato's sense, narration rather than dramatization. That is, they address the audience. They are all forms which, in the pretelevision film, were largely avoided. But they are all important in television.

We have mentioned several respects in which television, live or filmed, has become different from the theatrical film. The use of narration may be one of the most important.

NARRATION IN TELEVISION. For half a century the motion picture, like the theater since Shakespeare's time, shunned narration. If narration was used, it was generally done apologetically.

In silent films, narration appeared in the form of subtitles. Some narrative subtitles became masterpieces of compression. Anita Loos, writing for Douglas Fairbanks, became famous for her subtitles and was widely imitated. Lewis Jacobs quotes a typical opening in the Loos style: "Old Patrick Spaulding was as good a golfer as his tailor could make him." * But the highest praise was reserved for producers and writers who did without subtitles.

In the sound film, the narrator has been used regularly in newsreels and information films. He has generally been an unseen entity, an off-screen or voice-over narrator. He has generally been a nameless, abstract person, but not always. If identified, as in a sportsreel, the narrator might be shown for a moment at the start of a film before assuming the off-screen role.

The first-person narrator has been used in a few feature films, and almost always as an off-screen voice.

Thus narrators, when used, have almost never been seen

* Jacobs, Lewis, *The Rise of the American Film*. New York: Harcourt, Brace and Company. 1939.

addressing the audience. An exception might be made for a War Bond or Red Cross appeal, spoken by a statesman sitting at a desk. On the whole, these departures from tradition have always seemed to film people inartistic, and an unwelcome concession to amateur do-gooders.

But now, suddenly, television was full of people talking to the audience: hosts introducing plays, characters narrating, comedians doing monologues, salesmen persuading, candidates urging, lecturers explaining.

Was it just a radio habit? Was it because explanations are cheaper than dramatizations?

Probably both these factors played a part. But more important, narration could do things dramatization could not do.

Sponsors of many kinds, and their needs, assumed an immediate importance in television. That meant more accent on promotion, education, propaganda. In these, we must remember, narration plays a more important role than it does in entertainment. Dramatization is important in seizing attention and enlisting deep emotions; narration in channeling these emotions.

The film world's traditional dislike of narration was part of its traditional avoidance of any overt promotional, educational, or propaganda role.

Television, having no box office for income, and having the tradition of radio behind it, easily accepted a role comprising entertainment-news-promotion-education-propaganda. These complex functions needed narration as well as dramatization.

Television producers also found that narration suited the home screen far better than it had ever suited the theater screen. The big face in the theater, asking you to support the Red Cross, never looked comfortable or natural. On the home screen he seemed plausible.

If he had the gift of naturalness, he could seem to be talking to the viewer personally—something much less possible via a large screen. In television there could be a person-to-person feeling.

Here was a bridge from the inward emotions of drama to conscious, face-to-face relationships. For television, narration has become an economical, acceptable, persuasive instrument.

Again the choice of personality is crucial. Associations can open switches in the unconscious, stepping up the power of the message. One narrator is believed. Another, saying the same words, is hardly heard—or is resented.

If this is important in news, where resistance is slight, how much more important is it in promotion, education, propaganda, where resistance grows progressively stronger.

But when the personality is right, narration can become, in television, more powerful than in any other medium.

Over television, quietly and informally, great men of the age have talked to us. A Robert Frost or Frank Lloyd Wright tells about his life and work. There is astonishing intimacy. Throughout the great man's life, few human beings have looked on his face so long and closely as does the television viewer during such a program. Here intimacy and simplicity help give narration the most dramatic impact it can achieve.

Such programs give us a glimpse of the potentialities of television in education. For educational television, while needing narration, also needs dramatic impact—and needs it cheaply.

THE SEARCH FOR ECONOMY. We have repeatedly emphasized costs of television. The emphasis is unavoidable.

Throughout the United States educational organizations face budget crises. They cannot afford the school buildings, equipment and personnel which they desperately need. Some look to television to solve this. Some foresee whole curricula by television. Some argue that needs for school buildings, equipment and personnel will be reduced thereby.

There seems no doubt that education should use the great force of television. But meanwhile budgets for commercial network programs deal in such figures as ten thousand, twenty thousand, thirty thousand, fifty thousand dollars for a single half hour program, live or filmed.

Alfred Hitchcock Presents . .	CBS	38,000
I Love Lucy	CBS	48,000
I've Got a Secret	CBS	17,000
Kraft TV Theatre	NBC	30,000
Lassie	CBS	27,500
Life Begins at 80	ABC	7,000
Lux Video Theatre . . .	NBC	37,000
Meet the Press	NBC	6,000
MGM Parade	ABC	30,000
Robert Montgomery Presents .	NBC	45,000
Omnibus	CBS	68,000
Our Miss Brooks	CBS	35,000
Person to Person	CBS	30,000
Private Secretary	CBS	37,500
Rin Tin Tin	ABC	29,500

Weekly program costs of various network television series, 1955–6 season, as estimated by *Variety*. Estimates did not include time charges.

To attack a budget crisis with such expenditures as this is of course unthinkable. Obviously program costs for educational television must be mere fractions of prevailing costs.

But the prevailing costs, remember, already seemed like shoestring budgets to the film producer.

What genius can devise ways of using the same medium, to the satisfaction of the same audiences, with a mere fraction of a shoestring budget?

The impact achieved by such simply constructed programs as NBC's *Interviews With Elder Wise Men* seemed to educational television producers a most hopeful sign. Perhaps the answer lay simply in great teachers, quietly talking to a television or film camera—that is, to a nationwide class. Surely nothing could be so effective as this intimate association with a great teacher.

But who are the great teachers? Where can we find them?

Millions sat spellbound as Edward R. Murrow on *See It Now* interviewed at Princeton's Institute for Advanced Studies an atomic scientist of world renown. But he happened to be under security attack, and this was a dimension in the program. Audiences were held to this program by the most personal of fears and hopes. Every inflection, every expression, was amplified by underlying feelings.

Most teachers do not have such associations. Most teachers have, for the general audience, no associations. They arrive at high levels in their professions by publishing advanced works of small circulation. A few are brilliant in small seminars, with students they know well. Can they be equally brilliant talking to a camera? A few can, others cannot.

When teaching is felt to be brilliant, it may mean that it is just right for a particular group at a particular moment. If mass-distributed, for how many others will it be just right?

Educational television has relied mainly on lecture, interview, round-table discussion: narration in various guises. Too often the impact has been disappointing.

Some narrators have brought to television the visual aids of the classroom: maps, stills, models, magnetic bulletin boards, flannel boards, chalk boards. With some subjects, these help the effective television teacher to be even more effective. The less effective are not strengthened by them.

The educational producer therefore gropes toward dramatic forms, in which success or failure will not hang on the showmanship and personality of one man and the associations surrounding him, but on script values.

Can dramatizations be accomplished with less-than-usual budgets? What methods can be used?

Here is a problem important not only to educational television but also to smaller commercial sponsors and to independent stations.

COST-SAVING FORMS OF DRAMA. Various cost-saving styles of drama have been tried, some with success.

Cameo Theater pioneered a type of drama using no scenery. Scenes were performed in bright pools of light surrounded by darkness. Such scenes were generally spotlighted from above and backed by dark velour curtains, which disappear into invisibility.

Scene-setting furniture may play an important part in such productions. A roll-top desk is the office of a country editor. A bit of counter is the soda fountain.

In such a production, a prop may have the value of a setting. It is the ice-cream soda on the counter that makes it a soda-fountain counter. The camera starts on the soda, then pulls back.

Plays must generally be written with such techniques in mind, or must at least be adapted for these techniques. Unsuitable for many realistic plays, the method may be especially good for history, in which archaic surroundings may be distracting as well as expensive.

While the method may bring savings, the savings may not be large. Lighting problems are enlarged and their solution may consume precious studio time.

Another technique which may on occasion bring savings

is scenery by *rear projection*. The actors perform in front of a large translucent screen, on which scenery is projected from the rear via slides or motion picture footage. The technique is occasionally used in network drama productions. When the emphasis is on realism, little saving is effected. The edges of the rear projection screen must often be masked by walls, bushes, trees, windows, buildings. Only in a short scene can the area of action be limited sufficiently to avoid this problem. But when symbolic backgrounds are used, large savings are possible. In a very effective drama experiment, the *Omnibus* series used cartoon backgrounds, all rear-projected. In another, old engravings were used.

Many commercial producers shy away from such methods. But they offer a valuable area for experiment.

Another area is the drama of actuality. In the various press-conference programs, a dramatic situation is established before the camera. There is drama also in many classrooms.

In a painting class, twelve students paint the same model. The result is twelve paintings having a technical relationship to each other, but widely divergent in what they say. What forces are at work in these students that make such staggering divergences? As the professor goes from easel to easel, discussing with each, we get a glimpse of what these differences mean. Here is the drama of character revelation. Can it be made to happen in front of a television camera?

There is drama in many community events: PTA meetings, union meetings, community forums. There may also be hours of dullness. Can one foresee the moments of drama and arrange for them to happen before a television camera?

The appeal of the special-events telecast is well established. Talent costs are reduced. But technical costs may be increased. Let no one deceive himself that this, or any other kind of television broadcast, can be done for next to nothing.

Video tape should do for television actuality drama what

the tape recorder has done for radio. Even then, television will not be an inexpensive medium.

Controls: Television

The traffic regulations mount. They include all those affecting all the other media, and more besides. New problems relating to individual rights, such as those involved in the televising of Congressional hearings, will not soon be resolved.

Meanwhile censorship wanes still further. It is impractical, and the legal bulwarks against it grow stronger. As we have seen, moves of film censorship boards toward television censorship have been defeated. The emphasis is increasingly on freedom from prior restraint, plus clearly defined responsibilities.

The Great Transition: Merger of the Media

We have noticed, in each medium, a tendency to become involved in the affairs of other media. Television has become the meeting ground of all media.

From the world of print, the press associations and wire-photo services soon began to serve television. Newspapers and magazines bought television stations. Magazines and books became story sources for television drama.

From the film world, producers became television package producers, distributors became television syndicates. Theater owners bought television stations. Theaters became wired television outlets. A radio-television network merged with a chain of theaters to form American Broadcasting–Paramount Theaters, Inc.

From the radio world independent producers, talent agents, networks, syndicates branched into television. Many radio-station owners became television-station owners.

Each medium reached for a variety of outlets.

Each medium promoted itself through the rival media. Major units in each became active in all.

The worlds of the four media began to merge into one huge, complex world:

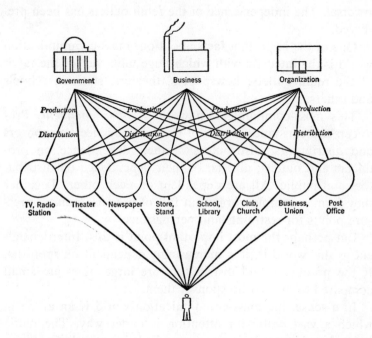

Let us consider this picture. It has many implications.

This mass-communication world is *huge*. It is inhabited by big units. Only big companies could have accomplished the expansion we have seen.

To demand an end to bigness is like lamenting the passing of the cracker barrel. The cracker barrel was democratic but the packaged cracker is here to stay. The democracy of the cracker barrel will have to be preserved in other ways. Hugeness is here to stay.

This mass-communication world is *competitive*. The big units, in spite of their size, do not control it. In each medium a trend to monopoly was reversed. Both business developments and government policies have played a part in this reversal. The independence of the retail outlets has been preserved.

One of the important facts about our mass-communication world is the intensity with which huge units vie for the favor of the retail outlets: newspapers, theaters, stations, schools and others.

This mass-communication world is *interdependent*. Producers are constantly aware of their dependence on sponsors and distributors; distributors of their dependence on producers and outlets; outlets, of their dependence on distributors and public. All are dependent on each other. Together they form a complex organism full of pressure points: pressure points for restraints and persuasions.

But perhaps the most important point is this. Interdependent as this world is, it is increasingly dependent on sponsors. If the producers and distributors are large, they are small compared to many who sponsor them.

In a sense, the mass-communication world is an arena in which a vast battle for attention is under way. The battle is fought with words, images, sounds. It is not only for attention but also for emotion. It is a competitive effort to channel emotion toward information, ideas, actions.

We all have a stake in this effort. We all identify ourselves with sponsors involved. The sponsors are business firms, government agencies, citizen organizations.

We now look at their work in detail: its objectives, methods, results.

BIBLIOGRAPHY: The Media of Mass Communication

SELECTED READINGS

Allen, John Edward. *The Modern Newspaper: Its Typography and Methods of News Presentation.* New York: Harper. 1940.

Barnouw, Erik. *Handbook of Radio Production: An Outline of Studio Techniques and Procedures.* Boston: Little, Brown. 1949.

Bettinger, Hoyland. *Television Techniques.* New York: Harper. 1947.

Chenery, William L. *Freedom of the Press.* New York: Harcourt, Brace. 1955.

Feild, Robert D. *The Art of Walt Disney.* London: Collins. 1947.

Greene, Robert S. *Television Writing: Theory and Technique.* New York: Harper. 1952.

Haight, Anne Lyon. *Banned Books: Informal Notes on Some Books Banned for Various Reasons at Various Times and in Various Places.* New York: R. R. Bowker. 1955. (Rev.)

Hyde, Grant Milnor. *Newspaper Reporting.* New York: Prentice-Hall. 1952.

Inglis, Ruth A. *Freedom of the Movies.* Chicago: University of Chicago Press. 1947.

Lazarsfeld, Paul F.; and Kendall, Patricia L. *Radio Listening in America.* New York: Prentice-Hall. 1948.

Manvell, Roger. *Film.* London: Penguin. 1944.

————. *The Animated Film.* New York: Farrar, Straus and Young. 1955.

O'Meara, Carroll. *Television Program Production.* New York: Ronald Press. 1955.

Reisz, Karel. *The Technique of Film Editing.* New York: Farrar, Straus and Young. 1953.

Seldes, Gilbert. *Writing for Television.* New York: Doubleday. 1952.

Spottiswoode, Raymond. *Film and Its Techniques.* Berkeley: University of California Press. 1951.

Spring, Samuel. *Risks and Rights: in Publishing, Television, Radio, Motion Pictures, Advertising and the Theater.* New York: W. W. Norton. 1952.

Stasheff, Edward; and Bretz, Rudy. *The Television Program: Its Writing, Direction and Production.* New York: A. A. Wyn. 1951.

Stefferud, Alfred (ed.). *The Wonderful World of Books.* New York: New American Library. 1952.

Vitray, Laura; Mills, John, Jr.; and Ellard, Roscoe. *Pictorial Journalism.* New York: McGraw-Hill. 1939.

Wolseley, Roland E. *The Magazine World.* New York: Prentice-Hall. 1951.

PERIODICALS

The Billboard. Cincinnati.

Broadcasting-Telecasting. Washington: Broadcasting Publications, Inc.

Daily Variety. Hollywood.

Editor and Publisher. New York.

The Film Daily. New York.

The Hollywood Reporter. Hollywood.

Motion Picture Daily. New York.

Motion Picture Herald. New York.

Printers' Ink. New York.

Publishers Weekly. New York: R. R. Bowker.

Radio-Television Daily. New York.

Television Digest. Washington: Radio News Bureau.

Variety. New York.

REFERENCE WORKS

(All issued periodically)

Broadcasting-Telecasting Yearbook. Washington: Broadcasting Publications, Inc.

Editor and Publisher Yearbook. New York.

Film Daily Yearbook. New York: Wid's Films and Film Folk, Inc.

The Literary Marketplace. New York: R. R. Bowker.

Mike and Screen Press Directory. New York: Radio-Newsreel-TV Working Press Association of New York, Inc.

Radio Annual—Televison Yearbook. New York.

Standard Rate and Data Service. Evanston, Ill.

Telecasting Yearbook-Marketbook. Washington: Broadcasting Publications, Inc.

Television Factbook. Washington: Radio News Bureau.

The SPONSORS
of mass communication . . .

SPONSORS, in the wide sense in which we are using the term, communicate with the public or portions of it through various methods: through space and time purchased from the media; through news releases issued to all media; through entertainment features in all media.

The communications of sponsors are aimed at the public through every available outlet.

The annual sums expended for these purposes in the United States by sponsoring organizations exceed ten billion dollars per year.

Since our nation was in its infancy, our media have always been sponsor-supported as well as audience-supported. But the audiences were originally the chief source of support. Today sponsors are the chief source of support. This does not make the sponsors all-powerful. Not all communications originate with sponsors. They originate at all levels, from sponsor to outlet. But the growing role of the sponsor does give him a far-reaching influence.

The problems of the sponsor depend to a large extent on whether it is: (1) a business firm, (2) a government agency, (3) a nonprofit, nongovernment organization. The problems of each will be examined separately.

1 The Voice of Business

Businesses invest in mass communication for many reasons: principally, because they feel they must for survival.

In most cases the original impulse is the promotion of sales

203

or services. If a business is close to its customers, as with a department store, it may see promptly the effects of its communications. But if the business is manufacture, the assessing may be difficult.

The days when every baker knew the eaters of his cookies and could talk to them belong to a distant past. Today's industrialist baker cannot talk to his consumers except through the writers, artists, producers, distributors and outlets of mass communication. He cannot listen to them except through sales charts, audience ratings, readership surveys, consumer-motivation studies, and reports on depth interviews.

More and more, users tend to become a great, remote abstraction: the market, the public. But the more remote they become, the more the manufacturer knows he must go on trying to communicate with them.

He knows this because, in our day, few condemnations of a product are more fearful in economic consequence than "Never heard of it."

Many people are sure they pay no attention to advertising. But they bypass with suspicion a label or package that sparks no recognition.

The larger a company becomes, the less it can trace particular income to a particular advertisement or program or film or brochure. And the less it dares stop trying to communicate.

If users become remote to the growing manufacturer, so does he to them. This makes problems.

Decades ago corporations became popular scapegoats. Size became synonymous with villainy. Remoteness helped this stereotype, earned or unearned, to fasten itself firmly on many companies.

There were other stereotypes. During the pacifism that followed World War I, former war-production contractors were regarded as "merchants of death." Could business, as a matter of survival, fail to take account of such stereotypes and to try to combat them?

We all use communication to shape, in others, a selected image of ourselves. We choose a tone of voice, a style of clothing. We modify our signatures. Companies began to do likewise.

During the 1920's, E. I. du Pont de Nemours & Company, Inc., widely thought of as a munitions manufacturer, although it made many other things, began to sponsor history dramatizations: the *Cavalcade of America*.

The broadcast series was promoted to schools and became "outside listening." A generation of history students learned from it. Starting on radio, it moved to television via film. The films, with a du Pont credit line but no commercials, were loaned to schools free of charge, postage prepaid.

Each version of history is different from every other version. Each version has a relation to its teller as well as to history itself. This may be only a matter of selection.

On *Cavalcade of America* all scripts were checked for accuracy by recognized authorities. But in the selecting of subjects and emphases, the sponsor made all the final decisions.

Wars were avoided. If stories did touch on war, scenes involving shooting and explosions were avoided. There were frequent stories on women's rights, and improvements in the lot of women. Unpleasant conflicts, involving labor or race, were almost never used. Stories of scientific achievement unrelated to war were used frequently. Commercials dealt with company research on "better things for better living through chemistry."

Thus, if a plan governed the selection of subjects, it was the plan of a new company image. This was institutional advertising, and it did its work. A new generation grew up with a new image of the company.

Though this began as advertising, it ended as classroom material used in schools. Was it, then, also education? Had the du Pont Company become a producer of teaching materials, like a textbook publisher?

Some people feel uneasy about such questions. But schools with tight budgets prefer not to ask them. If a corporation-sponsored film enriches the curriculum, and involves no direct product advertising, they welcome it. More and more, schools have begun to look to large corporations for a service no one else is fully supplying.

From General Electric, schools receive such brilliant films as *The Story of Light*, a history film with puppets and a musical score by the London Symphony Orchestra, produced in Holland under supervision of Transfilm.

From International Cellucotton they get *The Story of Menstruation*, with animation by Walt Disney Studios.

From Ford they get *The American Road*, vivid history of the automobile, produced by MPO Productions.

From Gerber Products they get *Mealtime for John Henry*, a film on child nutrition, produced by Wilding Picture Productions, Inc.

From the New York Stock Exchange they get *What Makes Us Tick?*, explanation of the stock market with animation by John Sutherland Productions.

Each year the proffered riches grow more astonishing. Available classroom aids include not only films but also filmstrips, booklets, comic books, recordings, charts, maps, teachers' manuals. Sometimes whole kits are offered.

Some companies have teacher-aid departments of several dozen people. Is it education, promotion, or what?

Some of the films mentioned above have appeared in

theaters. Thus they have made their way as entertainment as well as educational material. When *What Makes Us Tick?* opened as a short at a New York first-run theater, questionnaires were distributed, asking patrons how they liked *What Makes Us Tick?* A number of people considered it the best thing on the program. A few said they had come for entertainment, not propaganda. Was it propaganda?

In color animation (approximate cost: eighty-five thousand dollars), the film shows how a small investor, anywhere in the United States, can buy a share in a large company. It shows the operation of laws and regulations intended to protect investors. It emphasizes that ownership of many large corporations is spread over thousands of people, widely dispersed and including many small investors.

To people in Wall Street, these have seemed important points, helpful in combating the anti-Wall-Street feelings of earlier years. To tell this side of the story has seemed a matter of survival.

Was it promotion, entertainment, education, propaganda? The line is not easy to draw. Most kinds of business, at one time or another, are involved in touchy issues. A public position, a point of view, become essential.

Since the 1930's, views on current issues, implied or expressed, have played a constantly growing part in the communications of large companies.

Sometimes these views are implicit, as in history dramatizations. But sometimes they take the explicit form of *editorial advertisements*. Thus the railroads, in full-page advertisements, have repeatedly stated their position: that legislation has discriminated against railroads. On a number of occasions the Ford Motor Company, on the eve of union negotiations, has stated its bargaining position in a full-page advertisement.

Many advertising men have felt uneasy about this trend. Should advertising become involved in current issues, including such controversial matters as legislation and collective bargaining?

Media representatives have also felt qualms. Would the sale of space and time for controversy throw power to the wealthier side? Would the independence of the media be endangered?

On the other hand, who was to say that a company should not be allowed to state its case in a signed statement? Was the openness not preferable to hidden pressures? Besides, what wise man could ever draw the precise line between promotion and propaganda?

The communications of many large companies, in all media, have become inextricable mixtures of entertainment, news, promotion, education, propaganda.

DISTRIBUTION COSTS. The use of mass media by a sponsor involves: *production* of a communication—on paper, film, disc; its *distribution*—via various channels and outlets.

A century and a half ago the cost of any article was largely production cost. One result of the Industrial Revolution is that distribution has become a major cost ingredient. This is as true of communication, with its complex distribution channels, as it is of socks, frankfurters, hair tonic.

In communication, distribution is often *the* major cost ingredient.

Thus a sponsor, having spent thirty-eight hundred dollars on the artwork, models, plates of a color advertisement for a lipstick, may pay fifteen thousand for a one-time full-page insertion in a woman's magazine. From the advertiser's point of view this is a distribution cost: what he must pay to get the advertisement to a few million women.

Similarly a sponsor, having spent twenty-five thousand dollars on the production of each of a number of television films, may pay thirty-five thousand for each half hour purchased on a coast-to-coast television network. This, again, represents for the advertiser a distribution cost.

Locally, somewhat similar proportions hold true. Having contracted to pay forty dollars per week for local rights to a syndicated set of twenty-five musical weather forecasts, a local savings bank may find itself spending fifty dollars a week on broadcast time in which to use them. Again, a distribution cost.

When a firm produces a film to be loaned to schools, clubs, churches, the proportions are not very different. These outlets are available free, but distribution to the outlets is still costly. For example, the film *The Story of Human Energy,* showing via animation "how plant life converts the sun's energy into foods which the human body in turn transforms into fuel for action," is available to schools on free loan under the sponsorship of the Corn Products Refining Company. The loans are actually handled by the Modern Talking Picture Service, which specializes in promoting and distributing sponsored films via twenty-eight distribution centers, called *libraries.* This organization is reimbursed by the sponsor, on the basis of the number of times the film is used by schools, clubs, churches and other organizations. Charges made by distributors of this sort may average three to ten dollars per showing. A business firm, having spent seventy-five thousand dollars on the production of an educational film for free loan to schools, clubs, churches, may in five years spend fifty-five thousand to get it used.* Sponsors handling their own distribution may have comparable costs: shipping personnel, film repair, prints, cans, cartons, insurance, postage.

* *The Dollars and Sense of Business Films: A study of 157 business films produced by 67 companies.*

A printed communication, instead of going via newspaper or magazine, can be distributed as a direct-mail item. The cost, per person reached, will be higher. This may be worth while if the mailing list represents the ideal target audience.

Since distribution is so expensive, it is not surprising that companies seek ways to transfer this cost, or part of it, to others. A sponsoring company handles its distribution in one of three ways: (1) the company itself *subsidizes* the distribution; (2) it gets a *free ride distribution* by finding someone else to assume the distribution cost; (3) it arranges a *profit-making distribution,* getting someone to pay for the privilege of distributing the communication.

The examples so far cited are all examples of sponsor-subsidized distribution. Let us examine the other methods.

FREE-RIDE DISTRIBUTION. To get a free ride for a communication, the sponsor must shape it so that it serves the purposes of others as well as his own. If he wants his communication to ride free of charge in the news columns, instead of appearing at commercial rates in advertising space, it must qualify as *news* to the satisfaction of editor and readers.

For this reason, public-relations representatives are forever manufacturing events: press conferences, awards to contest winners, staged arrivals and departures, cornerstone layings, demonstrations, launchings, stunts. An astonishing proportion of modern newspaper content deals with manufactured events.

The fact that an event is manufactured does not in itself make it less significant. It may crystallize into one newsworthy moment an important trend that would otherwise pass unnoted.

The manufactured event has practical advantages over spontaneous events. Reporters and photographers can be on hand. Background material can be ready. Refreshments can be served.

Also, suspense can be built beforehand, possibly with some aid from subsidized communications. Rheingold Beer, with its annual Miss Rheingold contests, builds interest through paid advertising. Candidates are shown or heard in beer advertisements in all media. Through skillful management the contest builds public interest to the extent that newspapers and newsreels feel they cannot ignore the climactic announcements of winners—even of preliminary winners. These events are news.

Not only news value, but education or entertainment value, may be the basis for a free-ride distribution. A series of transcribed dramas on health, "based on the files of the Mutual Life Insurance Company of New York," was produced at the expense of the company. Because the company was satisfied with this brief credit line, the programs were broadcast free of charge throughout the United States, as educational programs "in the public interest."

Industrial films such as those used in schools may receive free rides on television networks.

The daytime interview programs are happy hunting grounds for free-ride promotion, based on entertainment or educational value. The author of a new book is delivered free of charge by the publisher, and the book gets free promotion.

Sometimes free-riders give free rides to other free-riders. The mistress of ceremonies of a woman's program on television introduces a film showing new spring fashions, as demonstrated by six beautiful young models on a Bermuda beach, hotel terrace, pleasure boat, airport. Where did the film come from? By what arrangements?

From:
BANNER & GREIF
369 Lexington Avenue
New York 17, N. Y.
MUrray Hill 6-6622

FOR IMMEDIATE RELEASE:

The Easter Bunny will come hopping around this year with his basket filled with even more colorful and imaginative eggs than ever before - thanks to the many-hued colored lead pencils which are now on the market. Of course, there is nothing new about colored pencils, but these are very special members of the writing family. Designed specifically to write on surfaces of all kinds, mothers and kiddies alike will find them the perfect instrument for turning the traditional hard-boiled eggs into a colorful Easter basket adornment.

These pencils, with soft, water-soluble leads, come in thirty attractive shades, certain to please every youngster trying his or her hand - and artistic ability - and may be used with no danger of puncturing or cracking the shell of the egg. They can be found at your local stationery store, but be certain you ask for water-soluble lead pencils. Of special interest to mothers, especially those with really young children in the family, is the fact that these colored pencils eliminate much of the muss and fuss of other egg coloring systems.

Instructions are as simple as this: just cover the surface of the boiled egg with pencil marks (either in solid colors or alternating colors), or possibly drawing designs such as an Easter Bunny. Then, with a dampened piece of absorbent cotton or tissue, go over the egg surface lightly. The water-soluble colors will blend into a smooth, evenly-colored surface, and "presto" - gaily colored eggs are ready for Easter morning baskets.

# # # #

Such a film was made available to television by Pan-American Airways. Its planes, having flown the girls to Bermuda, appeared in one or two shots.

Was it worth while for Pan-American Airways to finance this film? Yes: it did not have to pay the models. They were paid by the magazine *Seventeen*. *Seventeen*, wanting a spread of Bermuda pictures for its spring issue, got Pan-American

---

RELEASE—basic communication link. This release, sent out by public relations firm serving the Lead Pencil Manufacturers Association, was apparently liked by feature editors; it appeared on women's pages of hundreds of papers. Much feature material reaches the public by such routes. In form the release follows standard practice. For convenience in editing, editors recommend triple or double space—never single space. So that editor may add headline, it is sometimes recommended that release start a third of the way down on the page. On the other hand, inclusion of entire release on one page is a convenience factor, both for sender and receiver. The trade publication *Editor and Publisher* polled editors as to whether a headline should be included. The consensus: "This is immaterial." Some editors welcome a headline as an immediate identification of the content of the release. But sender's headline is seldom used, since he cannot anticipate editor's length requirements. If release runs more than one page, each extra page should start with new paragraph. Paragraphing should be such that final paragraph or paragraphs of release can be eliminated. If material is not "FOR IMMEDIATE RELEASE," release date and even hour should be indicated. For example: "ADVANCE—FOR RELEASE AFTER 2 p.m. Thursday, April 14." Source should be clearly indicated.

to provide free transportation. A copy of *Seventeen,* carried by a model, appears briefly in one of the shots. But *Seventeen's* main interest was in the still pictures, photographed at the same time.

Just the same, wasn't it all rather expensive both for Pan-American and *Seventeen?* Not really: a Bermuda hotel provided free accommodations; it appeared in several shots.

Hotel, airline, magazine all got free television distribution for promotional messages. The hotel and airline also got a free magazine ride.

Such exchanges of values, which the columnist Joseph Kaselow has described as companies "clutching one another in bear hugs and waltzing all over the terrain," have a long history in Hollywood. What car will be used in the feature film? An exploitation agreement may have settled this. The film will get free promotion in an automobile advertisement, showing the star and naming the picture. The car will get a free ride in the film.

American Airlines has long maintained, for free loan to film or television studios needing such a prop for a scene, a portable American Airlines ticket counter.

Are these trivial matters? To some businesses, tie-ups of this sort seem matters of economic life or death. Will the Hollywood stereotype of a rich home come to include wall-to-wall carpeting or shiny wooden floors? The answer may mean millions of dollars to floor-wax makers—or to rug makers.

In the 1920's and 1930's, the cigar skidded to near-oblivion. As cigarettes rose, hundreds of cigar manufacturers went bankrupt.

In the movies a cigar had become part of the gangster stereotype. It had lost all social status. Remaining manufacturers finally engaged public-relations representatives, and one of these concentrated on Hollywood. He made a trade: whenever a film included a distinguished man smoking a cigar, 25,000 cigar-store counters would carry a picture of this event advertising the film. Cigars began to get free rides in the mouths of heroes and men of distinction.

In another move, a cigar representative offered prizes to newspaper photographers: cash prizes each month for the best published pictures of men smoking cigars. More and more news pictures of important men began to include cigars, often provided, no doubt, by the photographers themselves. Cigars began to free-ride the news columns in distinguished mouths.*

All this makes sense only when we remember the part played in mass communication by the unconscious and its unrealized identifications.

Pepsi-Cola is the subject of an ingenious free-ride plan. The company sponsored a series of two-minute films on the *Perils of Lurine*. In animation, they parodied the *Perils of Pauline* cliffhangers of early motion-picture days. The films were designed for drive-in theaters, to announce the intermission and direct the audience to the refreshment stand. In many drive-in theaters, the refreshment stand provides the margin of profit. The zany films could do even more for drive-in managements than for Pepsi-Cola. They were glad to run the film without charging "screen time." As the trade press announced it, Pepsi-Cola made the films available "free of charge."

A free ride can be won not only for entertainment, news, promotion, education, but also for propaganda. Propaganda may be accepted because it is entertainment and education, as with *What Makes Us Tick?*

* Monroe, Keith. "They Made the Cigar Respectable." In *Harper's Magazine,* February, 1950.

Propaganda may also be accepted as news. In tense issues, statements of views may have considerable news value. The value is partly in what is said, partly in who says it. For this reason a public-relations representative, in promoting the interests of his client, may be mainly occupied in disseminating statements by others who are not his clients. This can lead to ethical problems.

The struggles between railroads and truckers offer a dramatic example. State laws limit the weight of truckloads, both for safety and to control road-maintenance costs. In the early 1950's, truckers were fighting for an upward change in the Pennsylvania load limit to bring it into conformity with that of neighboring states. The change was opposed by railroads, which saw the revision as diverting, annually, millions of dollars' worth of freight from railroads to trucks. The railroads held that trucks were already unduly privileged by riding on state-supported roadbeds, while railroads had to maintain their own.

A public-relations firm representing railroads logically sought co-operation from various groups in Pennsylvania and adjoining states. This resulted in many statements emphasizing public costs and dangers of truck transportation. For example:

(1) The New Jersey Rural Letter Carriers Association passed an anti-truck resolution and issued a release.

(2) The New Jersey Tax Study Foundation issued anti-truck releases and reports.

(3) The Empire State Transport League issued anti-truck releases, reports, brochures.

(4) The American Home Department of the New York State Federation of Women's Clubs held a forum and issued an anti-truck pamphlet.

Every public-relations firm stimulates like-minded organizations and co-operates with them. This is entirely fitting. But co-operation has many degrees. The possible range is suggested by the four instances listed above, in which the public-relations firm for the railroads was later shown to have played the following parts. It:

(1) *Wrote* the resolution issued by the New Jersey Rural Letter Carriers Association.

(2) *Paid for* the production and mailing of releases and reports sent out by the New Jersey Tax Study Foundation, "a fact-finding group."

(3) *Formed* the Empire State Transport League and supplied it with funds, because "we needed an organization that could legitimately mail all types of propaganda on the general subject of trucks and highways."

(4) *Paid a salary* of five hundred dollars a month plus expenses to the lady who issued the pamphlet and called the forum in the name of the New York State Federation of Women's Clubs—which later reprimanded her.*

The sponsor of a paid advertisement must, by law, be identified. The financial source of a free-ride message may remain a mystery. There lies the source of problems still unresolved. Where is the line between the proper and improper?

When the above activities were revealed and publicized, they boomeranged against the railroads. They may have helped passage of the load revision. Thus concealed sponsorship may also involve hazards.

PROFIT-MAKING DISTRIBUTION. Communications issued for promotion reasons may acquire value to the point where they can be distributed at a profit.

---

* Bendiner, Robert. "The 'Engineering of Consent'—A Case Study." In *The Reporter*, April 11, 1955.

When the *March of Time* first went on the air to promote *Time,* the magazine paid for both production and network time. This was sponsor-subsidized distribution.

In later seasons, the series returned under the sponsorship of Remington and other companies, still "prepared by the editors of *Time*." Still a *Time* promotion, the program was now getting, thanks to other sponsorship, a free-ride distribution.

Later the *March of Time* appeared in theaters as a newsreel. Still "prepared by the editors of *Time,*" still a *Time* promotion, the program was now distributed on a revenue basis.

The phrase "Inner Sanctum Mystery," devised by Simon and Schuster as a promotional slogan or trademark, acquired such value as to be a marketable commodity. When an independent producer first launched the broadcast series *Inner Sanctum Mysteries,* it was on the basis of a weekly royalty to Simon and Schuster. A slogan rode the air waves on a revenue-yielding basis.

The television series *Disneyland* was built by Disney as a huge promotion for his theatrical enterprises, yet having such high entertainment value as to attract sponsorship. This was promotion distributed at a profit.

COST SHARING: MANUFACTURER AND DEALER. The high cost of distributing a communication may influence manufacturer-dealer relationships. Often the manufacturer assumes the production cost of a communication, but passes some or all of the distribution costs on to his dealers.

The Texas Company produced, in 1954, a series of short films for theater use, showing scenic wonders. Production cost of the series was reported as forty-two thousand dollars. The films were made available free of charge to any local Texaco dealer; he could have his name and location added in a twenty-second trailer and could arrange local theater showings, at his own expense. According to *Business Screen,* dealers bought in one year four hundred thousand dollars' worth of local screen time for the series. Range of theater charges: two to twenty dollars per day.

Similarly a shoe manufacturer, such as Buster Brown Shoes, prepares mats of newspaper advertisements, with space for name and address of local shoe store. The store gets the mats free of charge, and generally shares space costs with the manufacturer.*

Relationships between manufacturer and dealer may be powerfully affected by the support each gives the other in these participation ventures.

COST SHARING BY RIVALS. The high cost of communication brings together competing companies, in projects for their common interest.

Thus rival California orange growers, having a common interest in promoting the consumption of California oranges, joined forces in co-operative advertising under the Sunkist trade mark. The Sunkist campaigns, starting early in the twentieth century, have used all media.

The expense of film has particularly encouraged this trend. Thus *Saugus Iron Works Restoration,* brilliant and authentic film on a New England iron works of 1650, was a co-operative project of iron and steel companies through the Iron and Steel Institute. The Institute distributes the film.

Professional competitors unite in similar projects. Tax accountants joined in a film of income-tax advice. Chiropractors joined in *The Chiropractic Story.*

---

* Some local media charge higher space or time rates to national advertisers than to local advertisers, on the grounds that national sales usually involve added commissions. This difference in rate may, in turn, influence the manufacturer. Instead of placing local advertising himself, he may prefer, by offering help to his dealer, to try to get his dealer to do it—at local rates.

COST SHARING THROUGH SYNDICATION. Local businesses which do not find their communication problems solved by manufacturers or co-operative arrangements may use syndicated *open-end* material. This is another way in which the high costs of communication—in this case both production and distribution costs—are shared.

Besides open-end recordings and films, there are open-end brochures, leaflets, calendars. Hardware stores throughout the United States send their customers at Christmas a "do-it-yourself" calendar, in which every page is a chart of carpentry advice and diagrams. A single hardware store could not possibly afford such a full-color calendar as a solo project. Yet it can purchase a few thousand, with its own name and address, at less than fifty cents each. Calendars of this sort are printed in editions of many millions.

We shall find the open-end idea penetrating into every type of mass communication, for every kind of sponsor.

COSTS AND THE CHOICE OF TARGET. For businesses, local and national, the cost of communication may influence the choice of target.

The first impulse of a business may be to aim its communications at the widest possible target. This may prove unwise.

The point may be illustrated by an experience of Carter's Pills. It originally took up radio network broadcasting after successful local tests. Local spot announcements, in many areas, had clearly increased local sales. It seemed likely that a network series of popular type would have the same effect nationally.

It decided on a new, proposed drama series, never previously broadcast: *Inner Sanctum Mysteries*. During the following year, the audience rating of this new series rose rapidly. It soon acquired the second highest rating on its network. Month after month, the sponsor expectantly watched the sales curve. The company continued sponsorship two years. The sales showed no significant ups or downs.

What was wrong? Audience and market research gradually provided an answer. Each week *Inner Sanctum Mysteries* was reaching a huge audience: of the young, strong, healthy. The program's taboo obsessions undoubtedly appealed strongly to them. Meanwhile Carter's Pills also reached a huge market: of the over-forty, unwell, worried. To them security was important, taboo obsessions no longer a problem.

Program and product each involved large population groups, but the two hardly overlapped.

Carter's Pills dropped *Inner Sanctum Mysteries,* which went on to do valuable service for other sponsors, on radio and television. Meanwhile Carter's turned for a time to a musical series. Its rule for choosing music: each number must be at least twenty years old. Featured with the music were audience letters, for which cash prizes were paid. Each letter told of the memories stirred by a particular song. For example: "Whenever I hear *Ah! Sweet Mystery of Life,* I remember how my husband and I once went to . . ." The series, titled *Keepsakes,* was thus a gilt-edged invitation to the unwell and weary to dwell in happier days. It never reached an audience comparable to *Inner Sanctum Mysteries* but soon stirred the sales curve.

A very narrow target may be the best target. The Federal Electric Products Company makes, among other things, a circuit breaker for the home. Replacing the old-fashioned fuse box, this provides the same protection without need for new fuses. The homeowner is the ultimate customer: a wide, expensive target.

Federal, a moderate-sized firm, could not afford to reach it. What did it do?

It invested $40,000 in a color film about its circuit breaker.

It never showed the film to a homeowner. It ignored commercial television and other huge-audience channels.

In each of hundreds of cities, a Federal salesman hired a dining room in the best hotel, and arranged a fine dinner. Only a few dozen people were invited: the electrical contractors of the area. Each Federal salesman was carefully trained in the staging of these dinners. They were partly social, partly business. He was the "master of ceremonies." Mimeographed instructions from his company included suggested seating plan, suggested opening remarks, suggested procedure.

The program included: (1) dinner; (2) movie, *The Stablok Story;* (3) invitation to examine equipment at side table.

On these small-audience sessions the company spent, in two years, far more than on the film itself. Was it worth it? At the end of two years, Federal was selling 40 per cent of the circuit breakers being sold in the United States. It had bet its investment on a hunch: that the advice of an electrical contractor, in face-to-face communication, is the most decisive factor. Federal put its full film investment into converting the contractor.

The Wool Bureau, representing wool growers, made a film to resist the effect of synthetic fabrics on their business. At what audience did it aim this film? To aim it at consumers might have meant a buckshot expenditure of millions.

In many cities, department stores and dry goods stores were invited to let their sales employees see, during working hours, a film which would help them to explain to customers the relative advantages of various wool and mixed-with-wool fabrics. In other words, the film was offered as an aid to in-service training, a tool for effective salesmanship. Again strategy was based on a premise: that face-to-face communication, between salesman and customer, would be the crucial factor in countless purchases, and that a powerful attack on the small target (salesman) would prove a better investment than a scattered attack on the wide target (customer).

Obviously, choice of target determines the nature of a film. Contractor and store salesman are focused audiences. The approach to them can and must be far more direct than an approach to a general, unfocused audience.

WIDE TARGET, NARROW TARGET. For the small promotion budget, a choice may have to be made. The larger the company, the less can it make a choice. A company like United States Steel, for example, uses the mass media to address those involved in every step of the complex process by which its materials reach the public. It addresses the companies that buy steel; the wholesalers, jobbers and retailers who market the steel products of these companies; the customers who buy them. It addresses stockholders, employees, government.

An approach to one of these may be planned for its indirect effect on another. In showing the public, on television, a particular kind of stainless-steel kitchen equipment, it hopes not only to stimulate the consumer but also to invigorate the entire distribution channel that leads to him.

In showing, through various media, steel fabrication in action, it is aware of the benefits to worker morale. In making its films available to school, church, club, library, it is aware of the possible long-range effect on young Americans.

Through its communications, the large company becomes involved in almost all segments of American life—even government.

BUSINESS-GOVERNMENT CO-OPERATION. One of the most interesting developments in mass communication is the process by which business communications have become free-ride vehicles for government messages.

During World War I many companies, having nothing to

sell due to war production, took up institutional advertising. Some featured war messages, while at the same time keeping brand names alive.

World War II saw a feverish increase in this activity, stimulated in part by government. Government agencies began to bombard advertisers with requests to feature this or that government message in printed advertisements and radio programs. Advertisers responded.

Meanwhile advertising budgets rose steadily. Some critics condemned this wartime rise in advertising as a huge waste of manpower, paper and other critical items. They demanded that companies not be permitted to deduct institutional advertising as an essential business expense. They pointed out that under high wartime tax rates, the money spent on advertising would otherwise go, almost wholly, to the government in taxes. They therefore claimed the public was paying for the advertising.

This dispute, rumbling in the background, may well have given an added incentive to *public-service advertising*— which government agencies meanwhile continued to stimulate with their requests.

In fact, the requests reached a somewhat ludicrous stage. The sponsor of a popular radio comedian demonstrated that if all government requests were granted, there would be no time for the comedian.

The situation led to the establishment of a government unit in the Office of War Information, to serve as a clearing house. Government agencies were no longer to make requests directly to advertisers or their agencies. Requests were to be channeled through the OWI. Meanwhile advertisers set up a War Advertising Council to work with the OWI, channeling the requests to advertisers.

This system relieved individual advertisers of the burden of deciding what requests to grant. The OWI determined priorities. In orderly fashion, government messages began to appear in business-sponsored communications in every medium. From time to time, advertising spokesmen announced how many millions of dollars' worth of time and space had been devoted to campaigns for war-bond sales, nurse recruitment, war relief, volunteers, salvage and other war purposes.

From the point of view of the position of wartime advertising, the development was momentous. The advertising business began to speak of itself as "the information industry."

Advertisers felt that the system should be continued in peacetime, in somewhat altered form. The War Advertising Council became the Advertising Council. Instead of a government committee to recommend priority of topics, a Public Policy Committee of prominent citizens from many fields was established by the Council.

Thus public-service campaigns, on such subjects as Better Schools, Higher Productivity, Red Cross, continued to be promoted in business advertising, as well as in space and time donated by the media. Campaign topics originate with government agencies or with organizations, but require the approval of the Public Policy Committee by a three-fourths vote, as well as approval of the Board of the Advertising Council.

The Advertising Council's statistics are always dizzying. It will report, for example, that during one year advertisers supported the CARE relief campaign with an "estimated 288,950,000 radio home impressions," the Stop Accidents campaign with newspaper lineage "estimated at over 10,850,000," a Religion in American Life campaign with "5,069 outdoor posters," a Forest Fire Prevention campaign with "25,437 mats . . . ordered for sponsorship by newspapers and local advertisers."

The Advertising Council urges advertisers to "sign" their public-service messages. Otherwise, in the words of Gordon Kinney, television-radio director of the Council, they are "letting millions of dollars in public relations for business go down the drain." In the *Advertising Council News* the following are cited as examples of how advertisers can sign their names to television or radio messages:

Remember, better schools make better communities. Good citizens everywhere are helping. This important message was brought to you by Libby-McNeill-Libby in the interests of public welfare.

So, in behalf of Swift and Company who donate this time, let me urge you to join and serve your Red Cross.

This is Del King speaking for Pet Milk Company, wishing you good luck and good health and reminding you that when you give to the Crusade For Freedom you give hope and courage to captive people behind the Iron Curtain.*

Leaders in government and organizations have paid tribute to the Advertising Council for the support given to their campaigns. There seems no doubt that the support has been valuable.

The campaigns are impeccable in purpose. They deal with causes that have solid public approval. If there is anything disturbing about the system, it is precisely this fact. The plan, like syndication, has a standardizing effect. It makes public service as ritualistic as a "personalized" greeting card. It also tends to create two kinds of causes: (1) approved, (2) others.

* *Advertising Council News.* May, 1954.

What this may mean to government agencies and non-government organizations will be discussed in our chapters on *Government to People* and *The Organization Speaks*.

BUSINESS AND FOUNDATIONS. We have noticed that tax policies played a part in the growth of public-service advertising. Tax policies have helped to build another, and probably more significant, link between business and public-service communication: the tax-exempt foundation.

Our laws permit tax exemption to nonprofit organizations set up for educational, philanthropic and religious purposes. High income taxes and inheritance taxes have encouraged wealthy men and corporations to give large funds to foundations. The Rockefeller, Ford, Kellogg and Sloan Foundations are among those which have interested themselves in mass communication, financing educational projects in television, radio, film, press.

The projects of the nonprofit organization may not, by law, be of direct benefit to the original donor. But indirect benefit is almost inevitable. Here again the indirect effect of mass communication, virtually unmeasurable, may be far more important than the direct. What emotional overtones has the name Ford acquired? The name was once associated with squeaky cars, anti-Semitism, union busting and crackpot peace schemes. Gradually it acquired connotations of power, liberalism, support to education, intergroup harmony and the arts. At the root of this change were deeds, but deeds which we know through communication. The rapid shift in the public image has been influenced by many kinds of communication. Company advertising and publicity have played a part. Foundation-supported television programs, films and aids to education have played a part.

Thus the communications of nonprofit organizations may serve as an extension of the Voice of Business.

THE CONSERVATIVE VOICE. On the whole, the Voice of Business exerts a conservative influence on the mass-communication world.

This is no high-pressure influence. It is largely indirect.

Decades ago there were stories about advertisers bringing pressures on newspapers, to secure editorial support for corporation views. Today one almost never hears of overt pressures.

However, in the selection of advertising media, most agencies automatically ignore publications representing fringe opinions. Such publications must generally survive on other kinds of sponsorship or on audience support—an increasingly difficult task.

In the selection of stories for a sponsored television or radio series, a similar tendency is at work. It operates all along the complex assembly line from writer to sponsor. Censorship by sponsorship is not exerted by the sponsor alone. It is more likely to be exerted by others, in the name of the sponsor. This is a problem for the sponsor. Underlings are often more cautious, often have less imagination, than the sponsor.

Here and there, nevertheless, powerful leadership cuts through the complexity. It may come from a writer, performer, director, editor, producer, advertising-agency man, or sponsoring executive. Business sponsorship has produced its classics, from *Nanook of the North* and *Louisiana Story* through *Theatre Guild on the Air* and *Meet the Press* to *The Story of Light* and *The American Road* to *See It Now*, *Omnibus* and the plays of Paddy Chayefsky.

All in all, American business has done well with mass communication. In terms of its aims it has done superbly. Government and citizen organizations, in contemplating their own communication problems, cannot help but think in terms of the accomplishments of business.

More than any other kind of sponsor, business has sensed the opportunities offered by mass communication, and has seized them. The organizations of mass communication have been shaped to meet the needs of business, and have met them.

During the past century we first saw business growing huge, in part with the help of mass communication. But while growing huge it also grew remote, and this made it vulnerable to criticism, fair and unfair. Much of this criticism was in the communication media. We then saw business, in self-defense, expand its own communication activities.

We saw the communications of business taking many forms: not only promotion but also news, entertainment, education, propaganda. Not only promotion of its own services, but also of government and organization services.

Thus through mass communication we see business permeating practically every phase of American life. Its communications reach the public through television, radio, newsstand, theater, store, school, club, church, library.

All this makes the old, pariahlike position of business and advertising seem a thing of long ago.

The advertiser, said Dr. Samuel Johnson two centuries ago, should be most careful. "He should remember that his name is to stand in the same paper with those of the King of Prussia and the Emperor of Germany, and endeavor to make himself worthy of such association."

In 1924, Herbert Hoover, as Secretary of Commerce, said something similar. He said it would be disastrous if a speech by a President were ever used "as the meat in a sandwich of two patent medicine advertisements."

Dr. Johnson could hardly have foreseen that before long, being King of Prussia or Emperor of Germany would not be as respectable as the professions of advertising and public relations. And Mr. Hoover could hardly have foreseen that within decades federal government representatives would come to advertisers, hat in hand, to ask for government messages in food, cosmetic, cigarette and drug advertisements.

The Voice of Business has grown strong. Advertising leaders turn senator and diplomat. Advertising men are consultants to Presidents and political parties. Advertising men have headed the Voice of America.

The business sponsor is the patron of our time.

Some people are fearful of this fact. They point to the excesses and banalities of much sponsored entertainment. Others prefer to point to its achievements. In all media, at all times, the treasure-to-trash ratio has been small.

Throughout history, the patron has sometimes put icy hands on the artist, and sometimes liberated him. This is the challenge to the businessman.

At first the businessman just wanted to sell his products. He was sure that was all he wanted. Today, for better or worse, he is leader, oracle, patron of the arts.

2 Government to People

The work of many government agencies requires use of the mass media. The reasons for using these media are as varied as those of business.

News releases, sometimes issued in press conferences, are important to the functioning of many agencies. Federal, state and local government releases are an important part of the content of most newspapers. Filmed and recorded press-conference statements play a prominent role in television, radio and theater news material.

Promotion is essential to the functioning of many government agencies. Often it is not enough to "offer" bonds. Government financing may require that they be promoted. For the control of inflation, low-denomination bonds must sometimes be vigorously promoted. Recruitment to armed services and civilian services must be promoted.

Entertainment plays a part in the functioning of some agencies. Through liaison with commercial producers on such broadcast series as *Treasury Men in Action, This Is Your FBI, Dragnet,* law-enforcement agencies at various levels have developed public images of themselves which are presumed to have aided law enforcement. Co-operation by the armed services on feature films, broadcast plays and magazine stories has had similar image-making functions.

Education has been aided by government use of the mass media. This has been largely a function of state and local agencies, but such federal agencies as the Department of Agriculture, the Department of Commerce, the Department of the Interior, and the Department of Health, Education and Welfare have supplementary educational functions carried out partly through the mass media.

Propaganda is an unpopular word. Yet propaganda in the best sense is essential to the functioning of many agencies. Many laws, passed over opposition, continue to be areas of skirmishing between government and citizen. Enforcement of income-tax laws, for example, requires more than the publicizing of rules. It requires rechanneling of emotional drives which too readily find satisfaction in cheating the government, heir of all father images. Timely revelation in the mass media of an important tax-evasion suit may play a part in government strategy. At the same time, other government communications may emphasize the paying of taxes as a privilege, or may deal with the use made of taxes. The propagandist applies pressure, while ennobling compliance.

In the light of the varied problems of government, it is

not surprising that its communication activities are huge. They involve government-owned production facilities and other facilities, in all media.

In each medium, government agencies have done pioneer work.

We have mentioned the federal government's war-bond drive during the Civil War: the largest advertising campaign carried out until that time. A short time before, in 1861, the Government Printing Office had begun operation. It has become the largest and best-equipped printing plant in the world. Some twenty thousand titles pour annually from its presses. Government agencies also use outside printers.

Film work was started by federal agencies as early as 1908, when the U. S. Department of Agriculture produced the first of its more than a thousand films. The armed services were early film producers, using training films in World War I. The federal government's vast, varied use of 16-mm films during World War II gave that field the biggest impetus it has ever had. Many state and local agencies have produced distinguished films.

Early stimulus to the development of radio, before and during World War I, came from the Navy, with its constant need for means to co-ordinate scattered units. The armed forces continued to be interested in all phases of radio. During World War II the Armed Forces Radio Service, a powerful cohesive force for troops at home and abroad, developed a network of over three hundred outlets served by transcription and short-wave relay. The armed forces were among the first to experiment with television as a training and co-ordinating medium. Many federal, state and local agencies have been active broadcasters, in radio and television. State-owned and city-owned stations have played a part in this activity.

In spite of all this, the Voice of Government in the mass media is a muted voice. Large portions of the public are hardly aware of the activities we have outlined.

There seem to be several reasons for this. One reason has to do with distribution problems.

We have noted that sponsors have their communications distributed in three ways: (1) sponsor-subsidized distribution; (2) free-ride distribution; (3) profit-making distribution. Let us examine government use of these methods.

SUBSIDIZED DISTRIBUTION. When one subsidizes distribution, one has some control over it. That is an advantage of subsidization.

One way to subsidize and control distribution of a communication is to pay for space or time in established channels.

Government agencies have to some extent done this, as in the sale of bonds. In a number of periods the armed services have bought newspaper space to promote recruiting.

But with the coming of new media, this advertising approach has declined. The mounting cost of space and time has been one reason. Another reason has been a philosophical one: the fear that purchase of space or time would seem, or become, a form of pressure. Another reason is the *public-interest* status of broadcasting. Should government pay, with public funds, for use of a channel which is supposed to be in public domain, and which government has made available for private-profit use without charge? Another reason has been the development of public-service advertising, offering a free channel for many government messages.

For all these and other reasons, purchase of space and time does not play a large part in government communication.

There are of course other ways of subsidizing, and thus controlling, the distribution of a communication.

We have seen how business produces films and pamphlets and makes them available to schools, clubs, churches. In doing so, it generally subsidizes the whole distribution process, paying for promotion, packaging, handling, insurance and sometimes postage. It pays for these directly or through fees to a distributor. For the outlet—school, club, church—the process is painless.

The shorter government leaflets, like those explaining regulations, may have a wide government-subsidized distribution. But more expensive pamphlets and films do not.

Most federal agencies producing films appropriate enough for production and a very limited number of prints. The number is likely to be especially limited in the case of those agencies—like the Public Health Service, Children's Bureau and others—that work mainly through state agencies. In the case of a Public Health Service film, for example, the budget may provide for fifty-odd prints. One print is placed on deposit with each state health department; further distribution of it will depend on state action. In addition, a commercial distributor may be given the right to make, and to sell or rent, prints of the film; his further distribution will depend on sales and rentals.

In the case of government pamphlets, the practice is similar. The sponsoring agency appropriates enough for production and a first press run. Free copies are sent to appropriate state and local agencies and to certain libraries; 125 libraries receive copies of all pamphlets printed by the Government Printing Office—some 150 shelf-feet of pamphlets per year.

A school, or library not on the special list, can generally get a free copy of a pamphlet by writing to the Congressman representing its district. But free-copy distribution is always limited. A school wanting a substantial number of copies, as for a class, is supposed to buy them. After the initial free-copy distribution, the main circulation of the pamphlets, via the Superintendent of Documents, depends on sales.

We shall examine presently some of the problems this raises.

There are still other ways of subsidizing and controlling distribution. The state or city that builds its own television or radio station is in effect undertaking to finance not only production of programs but also the process of distributing them. Transmission and engineering costs are likely to exceed programming costs. States and cities that have undertaken such expenditures have done it in the conviction that the commercial channels will not or cannot, in the long run, give them the air time needed for an adequate educational service.

Most states and cities have not felt able to undertake these expenditures. They must depend largely on free-ride distribution of their government programs.

FREE-RIDE DISTRIBUTION. As we have seen in our discussion of the Voice of Business, free-ride distribution can take many forms. The communications of a government agency, like those of business, win a free ride by their validity as news, entertainment, or education; or by serving the promotion or propaganda needs of others.

Free rides in the printed media are obtained by government through: press releases, press conferences, speeches, interviews, tips to columnists, letters to the editor, photo releases, assistance to writers and editors on articles and books, assistance to writers on fiction "based on the files" of the agency, assistance to comic-book writers and artists on comics featuring government messages, liaison with the Advertising Council.

Free rides in the motion-picture field are obtained through

many of these devices and through: ceremonies of interest to newsreels; help to producers through film footage in possession of the agency; help to feature producers in providing government settings for location scenes, such as Army camps, naval vessels, government buildings; research help on films "based on the files" or "produced with the assistance" of government agency; arrangements whereby a short government film is spliced to, and distributed with, a feature film.

Free rides in television and radio are obtained through many of these devices and also through: booking government spokesmen on broadcast interviews, panels, debates, round tables, press conferences, quizzes, variety hours, news programs; booking of government films or recordings on network programs; use of government stock footage on television programs; liaison on commercial series "based on the files" of the government agency; remote pickups from government settings.

It will be noted that government communications can be injected into almost every part of the production-distribution-outlet pattern of our mass media. The variety of techniques, and ways of using them, is almost limitless.

Consider the growing institution of the footage library. This method is used, among others, by the U. S. Atomic Energy Commission.

Early in its history the Commission began getting requests for access to atomic installations for the production of films and programs. It could seldom comply with these. But to leave producers to their imaginations was risky. One reason for helping was to keep a rein on speculation and rumor.

The Atomic Energy Commission therefore arranged for the photographing, by Signal Corps cameramen, of one hundred thousand feet of black-and-white film showing activities and equipment at fourteen installations of the AEC and its contractors. The footage showed, in long shot, medium shot, closeup, almost everything of interest that could be revealed. The impressive collection was made available to producers in 1952. Additions are made from time to time. To use material, a producer pays only laboratory costs of duplicating what he wants. He pays no royalty.

<u>Radiation Laboratory, Berkeley -- (L)</u>
(Reel 6)

No. 92:   (Radiation Laboratory, Berkeley: Biological Investigations with the 184" Cyclotron) Int., Close Shot of male Biologist using the microphone to contact the Counting Room (to tell them to arrange for irradiation of the rat). (Intercut for last part of No. 88.)

No. 93:   (Radiation Laboratory, Berkeley: Biological Investigations with the 184" Cyclotron) Int., Long Shot, high angle, of the Pencil Beam stand in the Deuteron Cave. The rat is in position on the holder. No personnel; no X-ray film plate. (This shot represents the irradiation of the animal alone.)

No. 94:   (Radiation Laboratory, Berkeley: Biological Investigations with the 184" Cyclotron) Int., Medium Shot of Pencil Beam apparatus in Deuteron Cave. The rat is in place on the stand being irradiated. No personnel. No X-ray film. (This is a closer view of No. 93.)

No. 95:   (Radiation Laboratory, Berkeley: Biological Investigations with the 184" Cyclotron) Int., Close Up of rat on stand. No personnel. No X-ray plate. (Closer view of No. 94, during the period of irradiation of the rat.)

CATALOGUE DESCRIPTIONS of U. S. Atomic Energy Commission stock film footage. Available footage includes thousands of shots. After studying descriptions, producer can examine selected footage on a viewer.

Thus anyone needing footage on nuclear reactors, particle accelerators, radio isotope production, radiation detection, or production of fissionable material, can apply to the AEC. If the intended film use is approved, the producer can study descriptive catalogues, look at footage on a viewer, and order what he needs.

The footage has been used by producers to make complete educational programs for television. It has been used in local and network news telecasts. It appears in newsreels. It is used for scene-setting shots, rear-projected background shots and transitional shots in film and television dramas. It is used as illustrative material in television lectures, and in appearances by scientists on interview programs. In short, through many channels it gives the citizen a look at important work which he is supporting. It may be considered a continuing report to the public, portions of which get free rides in various distribution channels.

An incidental result is that producers, to obtain footage, are constantly submitting scripts to the AEC. Thus the AEC has opportunity to correct errors and exaggerations.

PROFIT-MAKING DISTRIBUTION. As we have seen, many government pamphlets are sold. Prints of films are rented or sold. For many individual items, income may exceed costs.

But this seldom benefits the producing agency—for several reasons.

Revenue from pamphlets sold by the Superintendent of Documents does not go to the producing agency. Income cannot therefore be used to finance further communications. States have similar restrictions.

In the case of government films distributed by private firms, the government agency cannot demand a royalty. A successful film cannot therefore finance a new film.

The only escape, or partial escape, from this restriction is for the government agency to require the private distributor to devote net revenue to a specific purpose: such as another project in the same subject area. In other words, the revenue is used as a *revolving fund*.

Films or programs carried out with the co-operation of a local police department may result in donations to a police welfare fund, but not necessarily as a contractual obligation.

Except for these indirect benefits, the government agency cannot usually derive benefit from sale or rental income. A chief result of sale and rental arrangements may be to limit distribution. This is especially true when similar business-sponsored items are available.

For example, the U. S. Department of Agriculture offers *Meat for Thrifty Meals* as one of its "popular pamphlets" on home economics. The pamphlet is printed in small type on closely packed pages, without color. Its availability is announced in severe-looking price lists. *Meat for Thrifty Meals* sells at twenty cents per copy.

What similar material is offered from business sources? Every home-economics teacher receives promotion material from Audio-Visual Associates offering to lend—*free*—a set of three filmstrips on *How To Buy Meat,* sponsored by Swift and Company. With each filmstrip the distributor will send a *free* teacher's guide and a supply of *free* booklets, one per student—"to be kept and used as a permanent part of each student's library." If a school or school system would like a set of the filmstrips permanently for its film library, a gift set will be sent *free,* postage prepaid. *Free* booklets for new students will be presented each year. All the material is in color.

Such lavish offerings probably reduce the demand for the U. S. Department of Agriculture's twenty-cent pamphlet, *Meat for Thrifty Meals.* Its advice on meat is less likely to reach the consumer than Swift's advice.

DISTRIBUTION DILEMMA. On the whole, mass communication for the government agency involves a distribution dilemma. The agency cannot usually subsidize distribution. Sale and rental charges raise distribution barriers.

Most federal agencies therefore make materials "available," rather than promoting or distributing them. Most have a very incomplete distribution machinery.

There are some exceptions or partial exceptions. The U. S. Department of Agriculture, through its Extension Service, has a wide distribution network. The Social Security Administration reaches directly into the community. But even these depend, in the end, on communication outlets over which they have no control, and which serve them as a favor, not as a business.

As competition for these outlets becomes more severe, government communication with the public becomes more precarious. This is what the buyer's market—in words, sounds, images—means to the government agency.

BUSINESS LIAISON. It is not surprising that government has depended increasingly on liaison with the Voice of Business.

Many government agencies conduct important research—on nutrition, erosion, old age, crop pests, radiation hazards and thousands of other subjects. Many valuable government communications deal with the findings of such research. Some are of specialized interest, others of potential importance to millions. But perhaps those millions can best be reached not through a "for sale" item, backed by an inadequate promotion budget, but rather through a project like *Clean Waters,* a film sponsored by General Electric and produced with the co-operation of the U. S. Public Health Service. It is shown in thousands of schools, clubs and businesses—courtesy of General Electric.

If millions of farmers are to receive timely market information, perhaps it can be done best through the *National Farm and Home Hour,* which brings the farmer U. S. Department of Agriculture reports over a nationwide network—courtesy of Allis-Chalmers.

If school children are to learn something of government finance problems and the importance of savings stamps and bonds, perhaps it can be done best not through government effort but through a special *Lassie* film, blessed by the U. S. Treasury and widely distributed to schools—courtesy of Campbell Soups.

Such projects, subsidized by business, perform vast service to communication between government and citizen. As examples of business-government co-operation, they are of historic interest. But we should be aware of the implications.

In no other major country is government so dependent on channels controlled or subsidized by others.

In every other major country, government agencies can address the people through a government broadcasting system. In the United States, the federal government can address the people only through commercial networks.

In every other major country, government is the chief producer of educational films. Planned on a long range basis, the films flow into schools and adult-education groups in a steady stream. In the United States, government films are an irregular trickle reaching high quality but flowing through uneven, obstructed channels.

Government pamphlets, too, have an obstructed flow. Valued by researchers, little known to those who need them most, many lie entombed in library pamphlet boxes.

Our federal government has no assured communication channels to the public. In emergencies it can commandeer available channels. At other times it asks for them. Unlike business, it usually cannot buy them.

Those who handle the communication problems of federal agencies are constantly aware of all this. They are also aware that it is related to something we value most: our federal system of government.

Under this system, such important matters as education, health, child welfare are under local and state control. State and local agencies have jurisdiction.

Few would wish to change this. But in our age of mass communication, it raises problems.

State and local government agencies need the aid of mass communication. Schools and school systems, preparing students for an increasingly complex world, cannot do without it. Adult-education services, called on for lifelong education, cannot do without it. Health agencies, faced with the rise of chronic diseases and the need for preventive education, cannot do without it. Welfare agencies, coping with unrest and delinquency, cannot do without it. Our democratic system depends on an informed public, impossible without the mass media.

But state and local agencies can seldom afford these media except on the level of narration: talks, interviews, releases. These may reach the focused but not the unfocused. And the unfocused most need to be reached. This requires dramatic techniques which the local agency can least afford.

Using tax funds, schools and local health agencies in various areas cannot—like chiropractors, tax accountants, orange growers—pool their resources to solve communication problems. Most must rely on what services are offered. They become primarily *outlets* rather than sponsors or producers.

Outlets for what?

Clearly a wide variety of communications, under a large range of sponsorships, flows through the nation's classrooms and clinics. In school, students may learn history not only from teacher and textbook but also from:

(1) Television programs for classroom use such as the *District of Columbia Public School Series* over WNBW-TV, commercially sponsored by the Perpetual Building Association of Washington and used as an official part of the school curriculum, preceded and followed by the sponsor's announcements on thrift.

(2) Television programs from noncommercial stations such as Pittsburgh's WQED, the programs being largely nondramatic, some of them supplied by the Educational Television and Radio Center, established with funds originating with the Ford Foundation.

(3) Films by Ford, General Motors, du Pont, Standard Oil of New Jersey and other business sponsors, usually obtained by the school on loan.

(4) Films from Teaching Film Custodians, excerpting Hollywood features for classroom use as a service of the Motion Picture Association of America, the major producers—bought by the school system at a nonprofit rate, or rented from a film library.

(5) Films from Encyclopaedia Britannica Films, McGraw-Hill and other text-film producers—bought by the school system or rented from a film library.

(6) Films, few in number, from government agencies and universities, obtained through various possible channels.

(7) Radio programs broadcast for classroom use by Board of Education stations in various cities, often with student talent.

(8) Pamphlets, books, comic books from many sources, some obtained free.

Of course authenticity, effectiveness, price—all play a part in the school's selection of materials.

To some people, the variety of sources may seem woefully confusing; to others, wonderfully democratic. For better or worse it makes the school another mass communication supermarket. To a lesser extent, the same is true of clinics and other local-government communication outlets.

How does this affect the federal agency with educational functions? Controlling no outlets, seldom able to subsidize distribution, it has difficulty doing its job except through partnership with others: custodians of the media, business sponsors, organizational sponsors. If the word reaches a wide public, it is often through them.

Partnerships have their beauty. What could be more desirable than a system that brings government into constant collaboration with businesses and nonprofit organizations? What could be more desirable than a system which impels them to speak together, in unison, whenever possible?

But partnerships also have limitations. For one thing, they involve veto problems.

VETOES BY GOVERNMENT. The government agency is constantly in the position of wooing the mass media, then hushing up when they pry too closely.

This problem is inherent in every press release, every press conference. Each is an invitation to writers to pry beyond the mimeographed handout. That writers should do this, in our age of competitive communication, is inevitable. That government agencies should have matters on which they are not prepared to speak is equally inevitable.

Most government agencies have files which, in obligation to individual citizens, they cannot disclose. Most government agencies, like most businesses, have unresolved problems which they are discussing or debating behind closed doors. Public announcements say little of these. Public announce-

ments must deal with matters on which decisions have been
reached.

To say nothing of unresolved problems is not only natural;
it is often the only way to make progress toward solutions.
But to the newsman it is apt to mean: "They're hiding something."

A by-product of this problem is the *off-the-record* revelation. In this device, a development of mass communication,
the spokesman reveals information confidentially to newsmen on the understanding that they will not publish it.

Newsmen resent but cannot resist this institution. They
cannot resist the glimpse behind the scenes. But they resent
the fact that it ties their hands on things they might have discovered anyway. To them it often seems like censorship. (As
we have seen, censorship is to some extent inherent in all
sponsorship. The sponsor selects.)

Undoubtedly, the device is at times misused, concealing
what should be revealed. But it is a device that the media
themselves have helped to create, and that often serves a
valuable purpose.

Another instrument of concealment is the classifying of
government documents as *confidential, secret, top secret*.
These classifications are meant for matters which must be
concealed for national security. Undoubtedly this device too
is misused: to avoid embarrassment rather than to protect
security. This too leads to charges of government censorship.

When government makes available, for private use, government case histories, government settings, government film
footage, it must naturally examine the scripts to be used,
and request the correction of errors. This, too, may seem like
censorship.

The charges, true or false, seem an inevitable product of

government's constant and necessary liaison with independent media. Co-operation creates these veto problems.

But they may also work in the opposite direction.

GOVERNMENT VETOED. In its dependence on independent channels, government may be subject to their veto.

While the purposes of government communications often coincide with those of the media or of business sponsors, they sometimes do not.

For example, one of the government campaigns selected for emphasis by the Office of War Information in 1945 was on venereal disease. The campaign information, prepared by the Public Health Service, was relayed to the War Advertising Council. It was approved. Magazine advertisements and other materials were prepared by a leading advertising agency. Meanwhile angry opposition developed within the Council. Protesting memoranda were circulated, condemning the campaign as "intellectually immoral," a threat to advertising "as an institution." At the last moment, the campaign was reconsidered and canceled by the Council.

The protests, forcefully presented, may have had merit. The point is: the incident shows one possible outcome of the free-ride system of communication. In this case it resulted in business veto of a government message.

To the extent that business shoulders the communication problems of government, our people are fortunate. To the extent that this creates increasing dependence on such methods, communication lines between government and people are dangerously thin.

If we pursue this case history further, we find that while the system has roadblocks, it also has alternate routes. It is flexible. The campaign was carried through by other means, depending more on organizational sponsors—as well as on subsidized distribution and profit-making distribution.

This drive illustrates so clearly some of the problems of government communication that we shall review it further.

COST OF IGNORANCE. The campaign was based not merely on an agency proposal but on a decision of Congress.

In 1943 experimentation at a government research laboratory on Staten Island, New York, showed that penicillin could cure syphilis in a few days. Until then the prevailing treatment took at least eighteen months and was painful and dangerous.

The discovery had dramatic implications. Public-health officials had long held the opinion that several million people in the United States had syphilis—most of them without knowing it. Selective-service blood tests were confirming this. One element in this situation was widespread ignorance. Most people had no idea that the early symptoms of syphilis always disappear of their own accord, even without treatment; and that this may be followed by an outwardly symptomless period of ten, fifteen or twenty years.

The ignorance was costly. The symptomless period may be followed by blindness, insanity or other disastrous effects. By the early 1940's the United States Government was spending about twenty million dollars per year supporting the syphilitic blind and insane in public institutions. Each year the bill was rising. Syphilis was also a leading cause of death.

Surgeon General Thomas H. Parran of the Public Health Service insisted that the hush-hush attitude was contributing to this mounting horror. If the mass media would publish the facts, he maintained, so that numbers of people would volunteer for blood tests, thousands of the symptomless cases could be found and treated. Thus early candidates for public institutions could be reduced in number, with expectation of large federal savings. The advent of penicillin gave new force to this idea.

All this contributed to a Congressional decision: a huge manhunt, to be aided by education. Federal aid was to stimulate case-finding drives by state and local agencies.

TABOO PROBLEM. Of course this raised questions of taboo. The Hollywood code banned the subject. Most radio stations considered it highly dangerous; a scheduled network talk by Surgeon General Parran had on one occasion been canceled because he refused to omit a passage on syphilis. No large-circulation magazine had mentioned the word until 1937, when the *Reader's Digest* had broken the ice; most still avoided the subject.

Still, if the job was to be done, it could not be done through leaflets in clinic racks. The people to be reached were not coming to clinics. The word had to find them. Aggressive use of the mass media was needed.

For these reasons, many organizations were now invited to take part in the campaign. In spite of the reluctance of advertising agencies and others, there was willingness on the part of universities, religious groups, unions, parent-teacher associations, independent producers and others.

Columbia University Press, with a revolving fund at first government-financed, began to syndicate open-end transcriptions, films and printed material to state and local health agencies. Aided by federal funds, these could buy materials and distribute them vigorously to local outlets. The first transcriptions were brought to local radio stations with a message from Dwight D. Eisenhower as President of the University: "The American people must learn of the menace and cost of venereal disease and of their opportunity to eradicate it . . . radio with its impressive record of accomplishment in the public interest can be one of the most potent factors. . . ." Religious leaders had aided the preparation of the recordings. Under this impact the taboo crumbled. Over a thousand stations broadcast the programs—and heard no protests.

TARGET PROBLEM. But what were the results? Could the drive reach the target audience—those most difficult to reach?

The first group of programs included, for testing purposes, many different types. Besides talks there were three dramatic types: (1) straight drama, with radio and movie stars; (2) actuality drama, using tape-recorded interviews with patients under treatment (3) ballad drama, with dialogue scenes but with *narration sung by a hillbilly singer*. This third type, an extended singing commercial, was tried because of research findings on the singing commercial.*

Questions to patients in the clinics presently revealed a startling fact. Every ballad drama had brought to treatment twice as many patients as any straight drama, and four times as many as any actuality drama—all broadcast in comparable periods. Talks had had no noticeable effect. These findings led to production of more music-drama programs, starring hillbilly singers and gospel singers, and to the juke-box record *That Ignorant, Ignorant Cowboy*, sung by Tom Glazer.

Results: one state, Tennessee, estimated that during 1949, 18,032 cases in the state were brought to treatment through radio.†

One by-product was that *That Ignorant, Ignorant Cowboy* presently appeared under the Mercury label, on a commercial basis. Occasionally government communication receives this

* See p. 158.
† *Digest of Proceedings,* Ninth Semi-Annual Venereal Disease Control Seminar, Public Health Service. 1950.

curious, ultimate seal of approval: commercial distribution.

But commercial distribution could not solve all problems. Parts of the rural South could be reached neither by radio nor by jukebox. Here the answer was a film, with *distribution subsidized.*

The film was *Feeling All Right,* produced under Mississippi Health Department sponsorship by the Southern Educational Film Production Service of Athens, Georgia. Aided by federal funds, states bought over four hundred 16-mm prints of this brilliant film and kept it in constant, subsidized circulation for two years or more. In virtually every Southern county during this period, one or more state or local government employes continually arranged showings of the film, always with facilities for blood tests. Showings, always free, were in schools, churches, meeting halls. Discussion followed. Free comic books or leaflets, re-enforcing the message, were distributed afterwards. Blood tests, held nearby, continued several days after each showing. In 35 mm the film was also offered to theaters throughout the state and eagerly used. In every state, tens of thousands were brought to treatment. Such communication methods helped bring the following national results:

Admissions of syphilitic insane to mental institutions dropped from 6.6 per 100,000 population in 1939 to 2.1 per 100,000 in 1951.

Deaths from syphilis dropped from 11.1 per 100,000 population in 1939 to 3.7 per 100,000 in 1952.

The irony is that government agencies can seldom pursue the methods used in this campaign. Because of shortage of funds, aggressive subsidized distribution is seldom possible.

Because of governmental inhibitions, it is often not possible to use the most suitable techniques.

What causes these inhibitions? There are several reasons for them.

GOVERNMENT COMMUNICATION: LEGAL PITFALLS. A rider to the Deficiency Appropriation Act of 1913, Section 54, United States Code, states:

> No money appropriated by any act shall be used for the compensation of any publicity expert unless specifically appropriated for that purpose.

To some extent this was a product of early suspicions aroused by press agents. Yet there are good reasons for the stipulation. Surely government servants must not use tax funds to publicize themselves or their accomplishments.

The fear behind the act goes further, however. It is the fear in Congress that an agency will, through the aid of communication, exert pressure on Congress. This is made clear in Section 201 of Title 18, United States Code, passed July 11, 1919:

> No part of the money appropriated by any act shall, in the absence of express authorization by Congress, be used directly or indirectly to pay for any personal service, advertisement, telegram, telephone, letter, printed or written matter, or other device intended or designed to influence in any manner a member of Congress, to favor or oppose by vote or otherwise, any legislation or appropriation by Congress, either before or after the introduction of any bill or resolution proposing such legislation or appropriation.

This too seems right. Surely government funds must not be used for such pressures. The difficulty is, what is forbidden is almost inseparable from what is required.

To promote compliance with any complex law—the Social Security Act, for example—requires forceful, effective presentation of its aims and benefits. Will this seem propaganda for the Social Security Act? Will it seem to be pressing for extension of the Act?

Any effective mass communication, such as *This Is Your FBI* or *Victory at Sea,* may influence legislation, as well as publicize government servants.

The thin line between the forbidden and the required is an ever-present problem. On the one hand, it can excite Congressional suspicion of any communication that has a strong public impact. On the other hand, it exerts a restraining hand on the communications of agencies. The safest communication, from one point of view, is that which passes unnoticed!

The thin line between the forbidden and the required encourages agencies to work, whenever possible, through the liaison method, in which government appropriations are less clearly involved. Government has become, of all types of sponsors, most dependent on this method.

In all government communication, it encourages a muted tone. This results in communication divisions with such titles as Bureau of Reports, Office of Technical Information, and Public Education Section.

It influences the general air of government materials, such as pamphlets and films. The pamphlets seem to say, "We are not influencing anyone, just making information available." Of course, many people are aware that they *should* be influencing someone. But the restraining pressures are strong, the tone is set.

There is one inhibiting influence not yet mentioned: the Joint Committee on Printing. This congressional committee includes three Senators and three Representatives. It acts as

"Board of Directors of the Government Printing Office." It is supposed to "remedy . . . any waste in public printing, binding and distribution of Government publications." It fixes standards of paper and printing.

The Joint Committee on Printing frowns on color, wide margins and *white space* in general. It does not like to consider such matters in terms of effectiveness. Its job is economy, which is easier to talk about. In the name of economy many publications are made ineffective and probably wasteful.

In a sense, the style of many government pamphlets is a holdover from another age. The Government Printing Office was founded when our country was optimistically struggling toward literacy. New public schools were rising everywhere. The free-library movement was starting. The printed page was regarded as the key to salvation. It was assumed that the information being stored in the new library buildings would surely, in the literate America-to-be, turn into knowledge in the average man. Why should this not be assumed? The reader had always sought the word. There was no reason to suspect that he would not always do so.

But in our time, books cannot afford to rest in libraries or bookshops. Books pursue the public into two hundred thousand supermarkets, drugstores, cigarstores, and from display racks shout in bright colors to the hurrying shopper.

Can the government pamphlet, which holds answers for many, afford to sit on office shelves, waiting for dimes and quarters to be sent in? Can the health leaflet afford to sit in clinic racks, waiting for the citizen? Can the government film afford to sit, almost unpublicized, in film libraries?

Too often our government communications reach the focused, and not the unfocused who need them most.

This is partly because of budgets, but also partly because

we seem to want it that way. For these many reasons the Voice of Government is, on the whole, a quiet voice.

3 The Organization Speaks

To serve needs not filled by private business or by government, Americans form thousands of nonprofit, nongovernment organizations. They are large, small, weak, powerful, quiet, obstreperous.

Many communicate with the public through the mass media. Their communications include entertainment, news, promotion, education, propaganda.

They communicate to carry out their main purposes or specific related purposes: to raise funds, secure members, stimulate adherents, persuade voters, influence legislation. Organizational uses of the mass media are as varied as those of business and government.

Some organizations are custodians of minority causes. Occasionally a minority cause, first urged by a small band regarded as crackpot, later reaches such acceptance as to become a function of government or business. Votes for women, education for everyone, child labor regulation, responsible advertising, old age security, control of racial discrimination, are among causes that have made or are making this transition.

While some organizations are thus self-liquidating, many are not. The success of the American Diabetes Association in furthering the survival of diabetics actually enlarges the job before it. As more diabetics survive, lead normal lives, have children, the proportion of diabetics in our population increases. Similarly the proportion of people with heart disease is increasing, partly because of the effectiveness of the American Heart Association in furthering research and education.

Neither government nor private business is anxious to assume supervision over such growing problems. Instead both government and business do what they can to help nonprofit, nongovernment organizations to cope with them—via donations rather than tax funds.

We are inclined to think of "causes" as beneficiaries of free space and time in the mass media. To a large extent they are, but to a large extent they are not. Many must, at times, pay for distribution of their messages.

SPONSOR-SUBSIDIZED DISTRIBUTION. Among those which must often pay for distribution are religious groups, political parties, unions. For example, they often buy television and radio time.

Most people are puzzled, even disturbed, at the thought of religious groups buying time like advertisers, to propagate teachings. Theoretically, many media leaders are against it. "A charge for television time to churches and religious bodies is not recommended," says the television code adopted in 1951 by the National Association of Radio and Television Broadcasters. Yet many religious programs on television are broadcast in time paid for at commercial rates. And according to *Broadcasting-Telecasting* magazine, more than half the radio time devoted to religion is paid for at commercial rates.*

There are reasons for this. Considering the hundreds of religious groups in the United States, no station or network could give time to all. Some broadcasters solve this problem by giving a limited amount of time to organizations representing major groups: Protestants, Catholics, Jews.

The National Broadcasting Company, for example, gives

* "Religion On the Air." In *Broadcasting-Telecasting,* November 15, 1954.

the Protestant allotment to the National Council of the Churches of Christ in the U.S.A., which in turn apportions it to meet its internal needs and stresses. The Columbia Broadcasting System has generally tried to do this apportioning itself, on the basis of group size, with some allowance for other factors.

Many stations have tried a similar policy: to *give* time to major groups and then say, "No more."

But the drawing of such a line between the big and the small, the established and the unestablished, involves philosophical pitfalls. Applied to religion, bigness and social acceptability are hardly perfect criteria. Hence the decision of many stations to open the door a little further—on the basis of payment. The financial problems of some stations have encouraged this development.

The money requirement does some weeding out. As a criterion for selection, this is no more perfect than size. But it has the similar advantage of being mechanical, and not depending on the personal judgments of broadcasting executives as to the relative merit of creeds. It makes a group establish its vitality in rather practical terms.

Thus the Seventh Day Adventists, to name an example, have been regular purchasers of television time over ABC-TV. Year by year they have expanded their time purchases. The same is true of many other groups, including some large and numerous small ones.

How can small groups afford it? The answer is, some have found that television and radio can win new members, increase attendance, stimulate donations, sell publications, build mailing lists for further membership and fund drives and thus, financially and otherwise, strengthen the organization.

The mass media, to missionaries as to salesmen, are door

openers. A letter to a broadcasting evangelist, thousands of miles away, may bring a ring at the listener's doorbell a few days later: the affiliated local minister is calling.

Successful application of mass-media methods thus gives further impetus to a system that still causes misgivings.

Many people are also disturbed about political parties buying time. Again there are reasons for the system.

During noncampaign periods political programs are often carried free by networks and stations. Political conventions and some other meetings are carried free, as news events. But during campaigns increased demands for time bring complex problems. Some of these are financial.

To clear time for a political broadcast, a network or station must often cancel a commercial one. This may mean more than loss of time revenue. Contracted talent may have to be paid, even though not used. Giving extensive time during campaigns could send broadcasters into bankruptcy.

There are also legal problems. All "legally qualified" candidates for the same office are entitled, by law, to equivalent treatment from television and radio stations. If one candidate for an office is refused time, all must be refused. If one receives time, all must receive time—on the same terms and conditions. Networks and stations solve this problem by applying full commercial rates during campaign periods. Again, the money requirement does some weeding out. Again, the yardstick has faults but has the advantage of being mechanical, and not depending on value judgments.

In practice, it usually means the small party gets less time than the big party. The right to buy just as much time may not mean much to the minor party. The system thus favors the large, or at least the well-financed party.

Any alternative plan would raise its own problems. The Columbia Broadcasting System has pointed out that in some

RHODE ISLAND

Providence—W J A R-TV—Continued

Cash in advance.

POLITICAL ✓

REHEARSAL TIME
Rates include transmitter, studio and film facilities, including necessary set-up time, but not rehearsal. Rehearsal time for live programs, at the rate of 50.00 per hour. Amount of rehearsal at all times to be determined by the station.
Film rehearsal included in normal rates up to one hour. Any time in excess of one hour will be charged at 25.00 for 1/2 hour or less.

REMOTE CONTROL
Two RCA Image Orthicon cameras, portable transmitter for video, mobile unit with truck giving complete coverage for indoor or outdoor remote telecasts.
Technical equipment.
For outside or indoor remote telecasts: (1) mobile unit, two image orthicon cameras, (2) microwave transmitter.

FILM PROGRAMS
(ID Specifications)
Accepts SRA 3/4 ID Standard
Accepts SRA full screen 8 sec. SB Standard

PROJECTORS
Film
4 film projectors (16mm).
Send only 16mm.

Slides
3 slide projectors.
2 x 2 tape or metal mounted (prefer metal).

Telop Projector 4" x 5" cards; safe copy area 2-1/4" x 3-1/4".

Logotypes
Call letters 1/4 upper right only.

Time Requirements
Materials required by station prior to telecast—
Film: 72 hours.
Slides: 72 hours.
Artwork: 96 hours.

STUDIOS
Cameras:
2 film cameras (16mm).
1 motion picture (16mm).
1 film studio.
Film editing service available.
Film processing unit available.

For studio telecasts:
Three Image Orthicon cameras, dolly mounted. Mobile cameras also available for studio.
Advisory services of station staff are available to sponsor without charge. Prices will be quoted on request for station produced programs. No charges for services of a staff announcer except when he appears before camera, rates on request.
Charges for cutting and editing film programs included in film rehearsal charges. The transporting cost of films shall be borne by advertiser. Artwork, set design, set construction, stage properties, props and related production services are available from or through the station. Rates on request.
Script mimeographing available at cost.

Closing Time
All program content and advertising copy, either script or film must be received at least 72 hours (exclusive of Saturdays, Sundays and Holidays) prior to schedule time.

WPRO-TV
(Airdate March 27, 1955)

THE BLAIR TV REPRESENTED STATION

Basic CBS Television

PROGRAMS
CLASS "A"
(7:30 p.m. to 11:00 p.m. Monday through Saturday; 6:00 p.m. to 11:00 p.m. Sunday)

	1 hr.	1/2 hr.	1/4 hr.	10 min.	5 min.
1 time......	1,000.00	600.00	400.00	350.00	250.00
26 times.....	950.00	570.00	380.00	332.50	237.50
52 times.....	900.00	540.00	360.00	315.00	225.00
104 times.....	850.00	510.00	340.00	297.50	212.50
156 times.....	800.00	480.00	320.00	280.00	200.00
260 times.....	750.00	450.00	300.00	262.50	187.50

CLASS "B"
(5:00 p.m. to 7:30 p.m. Monday through Saturday; 11:00 p.m. to 11:15 p.m. daily; 4:00 p.m. to 6:00 p.m. Sunday)

1 time......	750.00	450.00	300.00	262.50	187.50
26 times.....	712.50	427.50	285.00	249.35	178.10
52 times.....	675.00	405.00	270.00	236.25	168.75
104 times.....	637.50	382.50	255.00	223.10	159.35
156 times.....	600.00	360.00	240.00	210.00	150.00
260 times.....	562.50	337.50	225.00	196.85	140.60

CLASS "C"
(10:00 a.m. to 5:00 p.m. Monday through Saturday; 12:00 noon to 4:00 p.m. Sunday; 11:15 p.m. to 11:45 p.m. daily)

1 time......	500.00	300.00	200.00	175.00	125.00
26 times.....	475.00	285.00	190.00	166.25	118.75
52 times.....	450.00	270.00	180.00	157.50	112.50
104 times.....	425.00	255.00	170.00	148.75	106.25
156 times.....	400.00	240.00	160.00	140.00	100.00
260 times.....	375.00	225.00	150.00	131.25	93.75

CLASS "D"
(Sign-on to 10:00 am. Monday through Saturday; sign-on to 12:00 noon Sunday; 11:45 p.m. to sign-off daily)

1 time......	250.00	150.00	100.00	87.50	62.50
26 times.....	237.50	142.50	95.00	83.10	59.35
52 times.....	225.00	135.00	90.00	78.75	56.25
104 times.....	212.50	127.50	85.00	74.35	53.10
156 times.....	200.00	120.00	80.00	70.00	50.00
260 times.....	187.50	112.50	75.00	65.60	46.85

ANNOUNCEMENTS
Effective December 1, 1955.

CLASS "AA"
(8:00 p.m. to 10:30 p.m. Sunday through Saturday)

	(*)	(†)		(*)	(†)
1 time...	240.00	120.00	104 times	204.09	102.00
26 times..	228.00	114.00	156 times	192.00	96.00
52 times..	216.00	108.00	260 times	180.00	90.00

CLASS "A"
(7:30 p.m. to 8:00 p.m. Monday through Saturday; 6:00 p.m. to 8:00 p.m. Sunday; 10:30 p.m. to 11:00 p.m. Sunday through Saturday)

	(*)	(†)		(*)	(†)
1 time....	180.00	90.00	104 times	153.00	76.50
26 times..	171.00	85.50	156 times	144.00	72.00
52 times..	162.00	81.00	260 times	135.00	67.50

CLASS "B"
(5:00 p.m. to 7:30 p.m. Monday through Saturday; 11:00 p.m. to 11:15 p.m. daily; 4:00 p.m. to 6:00 p.m. Sunday)

	(*)	(†)		(*)	(†)
1 time....	120.00	60.00	104 times	102.00	51.00
26 times..	114.00	57.00	156 times	96.00	48.00
52 times..	108.00	54.00	260 times	90.00	45.00

CLASS "C"
(10:00 a.m. to 5:00 p.m. Monday through Saturday; 12:00 noon to 4:00 p.m. Sunday; 11:15 p.m. to 11:45 p.m. daily)

	(*)	(†)		(*)	(†)
1 time....	90.00	45.00	104 times	76.50	38.25
26 times..	85.50	42.75	156 times	72.00	36.00
52 times..	81.00	40.50	260 times	67.50	33.75

CLASS "D"
(Sign-on to 10:00 a.m. Monday through Saturday; sign-on to 12:00 noon Sunday; 11:45 p.m. to sign-off daily)

	(*)	(†)		(*)	(†)
1 time...	45.00	22.50	104 times	38.25	19.10
26 times..	42.75	21.35	156 times	36.00	18.00
52 times..	40.50	20.25	260 times	33.75	16.85

(*) One minute or 20 seconds.
(†) 10 second identification.

Announcements adjacent to higher rate classifications take the higher rate.

CBS Television Network standard cut-in charges apply. For murther information contact CBS Television Sales Service Department.

CAMERA REHEARSAL
Camera rehearsal charge—25.00 net per 1/2 hour or fraction thereof.

SPECIAL FEATURES ✓
News Service—UP, Movietone. Rates on request.

POLITICAL ✓
Regular rates apply; frequency discount determined by total number of broadcasts for individual candidates. Payable in advance.

REMOTE CONTROL
Programs outside of studios subject to additional charges. Rates and information on request.

SERVICE FACILITIES
FILM PROGRAMS
- (ID Specifications)
Accepts SRA Standards

PROJECTORS
Film
2 film projectors (16mm).
Send only 16mm, single perforated stock only.

recent elections more than twenty legally qualified candidates for President have appeared on the ballots. Free time for all would encourage this spawning of parties and candidates.

Thus the paid-time system, while causing misgivings, has become firmly rooted. It makes fund-raising one of the most necessary activities of any political group.

Among other organizations facing the paid-time problem are unions. Unions have often received free time. In the 1940's some broadcasting companies began giving equivalent periods to union and management organizations. But the time periods were often fringe periods, of minor value.

There was also the problem of station acceptance. *Labor For Victory*, an AFL-CIO series, was carried free by the National Broadcasting Company, which offered the series to its full network. But usually only thirty-odd stations carried it. Hence the labor decision, early in the 1950's, to control the distribution of its programs through purchase of time on a coast-to-coast network of stations.

The heightening competition for attention has thus en-

POLITICAL SPONSORS are welcomed with mixed emotions by the broadcaster, as the facing page suggests. For political parties and candidates the rule often is: *cash in advance.* Some broadcasters use a phrase with softened edges: *payable in advance.* Presumably it is hard to collect from a defeated candidate; at times it may be even harder to collect from a victorious candidate. Note: one hour of Class "A" time, in Providence alone, costs $1000. Paid political broadcasting represents a dilemma for the broadcaster, the politican—and democracy. Reproduced, with permission, from *Spot Television Rates and Data,* one of the periodical publications of Standard Rate and Data Service, Inc.

couraged time purchases. On the whole, the subsidized-distribution method is used by nonprofit organizations more than by government agencies—partly from necessity, partly from choice.

But this choice can be made only by powerful organizations, or those which can readily translate the expenditure into income—as some religious groups do.

FREE-RIDE DISTRIBUTION. Most organizations, unable to afford subsidized distribution, must rely mainly on free-ride methods. As we shall see, this once more favors some kinds of organization over others.

As with business and government communications, an organization message can get a free ride in many different ways.

It may be in the form of news issued in a press release: the National Association for the Advancement of Colored People from time to time releases to the press a letter it has written to the U.S. Attorney General, demanding action in a case of alleged rights infringement.

It may take the form of news emanating from a created event: Princeton University, celebrating its bicentennial, held convocations that became news springboards.

It may take the form of a television or radio program produced at the expense of an organization but carried free by a network: the National Broadcasting Company has given free distribution, as well as limited production assistance, to the *Eternal Light* radio series and to occasional special telecasts of the Jewish Theological Seminary of America.

It may take the form of organization liaison with a network project: the television series *Adventure* was launched as a CBS Television Network production with the co-operation of the American Museum of Natural History.

It may take the form of announcements organized through the Advertising Council: the work of the National Citizens

Commission for the Public Schools has been furthered in this way.

It may take the form of a film receiving free theatrical distribution: a series of animated films on economics, sponsored by Harding College with a Sloan Foundation grant, were distributed by Metro-Goldwyn-Mayer without charge to theaters or sponsors.

It may take the form of a magazine picture story suggested by an organization; or an organization pamphlet or film, distributed at the expense of a business firm or of another organization.

Locally, many of these same devices are used. There may also be some method of dividing production costs among various local units.

Thus community chests and councils in all parts of the United States receive free time and space in many media. To help them make good use of this time and space, as well as for other reasons, they formed Community Chests and Councils of America, Inc. Headquartered in New York, it was set up with a revolving fund with which to produce open-end transcriptions, films, booklets, posters, articles, pictures —for the use of the local chests and councils. The local units acquire these materials by purchase, thus maintaining the revolving fund. This is syndication on a nonprofit basis, helping local groups make good use of free rides in local media.

During noncampaign periods many politicians get free rides in local media. Congressmen, for example, report on their stewardship via newspaper columns, recordings, films. Political parties try to foster this by aids to showmanship.

For example, a Congressman's filmed talks on current issues, for television use in the home district, may be aided by special footage supplied by the party organization or by the joint House and Senate radio-television studio. The same footage is used by dozens of different Congressmen, each in his area, each with his own commentary. This is another type of open-end, syndicated service, facilitating effective, economical use of local free rides.

A local free ride may take still another form. A small church is approached by a calendar distributor, submitting a religious calendar showing the world's most famous religious paintings. The church would like to send such a calendar to its members at Christmas time but cannot possibly consider the expense. The salesman, undismayed, asks, "How many could you send, if I find someone to pay all costs?" Having received his answer, the salesman finds a donor within the hour. The calendars are imprinted:

THE FRIENDLY CHURCH AT PIERMONT, N.H.
Worship Service, Sunday 11:00 A.M.

Courtesy of
A. E. Hale Co., Funeral Directors, Bradford, Vt.
Dependable Service in Your Hour of Need

In the same way, a hospital sends out safety calendars through the courtesy of the local taxi company.

An organization wins a free ride for its communications by serving the purposes of others as well as its own. We see mass communication, again and again, stimulating interrelationships—locally and nationally.

But all this inevitably favors the noncontroversial over the controversial cause. It favors the established over the new. Few business sponsors will "waltz" with the controversial group. The implications of this will be discussed presently.

PROFIT-MAKING DISTRIBUTION. Sometimes an organization tries to communicate its message on a revenue-yielding basis:

through book sales, newsstand sales, rental of films to theaters, or sale of broadcast series to business sponsors.

A successful example was the film *Martin Luther,* produced by Louis de Rochemont under Lutheran sponsorship and representing an investment by the sponsors of five hundred thousand dollars. The film played commercially in thousands of theaters in the United States, returning to its sponsors far more than the original cost.

There have been many attempts at commercial distribution of organization messages. *With These Hands,* a film of the International Ladies Garment Workers Union, was offered to theaters on a commercial basis. *Negro Heroes,* National Urban League comic-book series, was sold through newsstands on a commercial basis. But few such projects have had the large-scale success of *Martin Luther.*

The income derived is only one of the arguments favoring this approach. *Martin Luther* is believed to have reached over twenty million people in the United States. Telling its story in powerfully dramatic terms, it reached people who would never have been touched by five hundred thousand dollars invested in less dramatic pamphlets and broadcast sermons. These narrations would have tended to reach, over and over, the already persuaded.

This is one of the dilemmas constantly faced by organizations. The key to wide distribution, large audiences, new audiences, is emotional identification. For the unfocused, this means dramatization. And dramatization means expense.

TECHNIQUE DILEMMA. In every medium we have found dramatization more expensive than narration. Unfortunately, the difference grows larger.

On the printed page, the drama of pictures costs more than words—*a little more.*

On radio, dramatic forms cost more than talks—*a good deal more.*

On television, live or filmed, drama costs more than talk —*an enormous lot more.*

The difference, growing larger, affects countless decisions. For an organization it may mean: "Shall we be content to address those already emotionally with us—as narration can do efficiently and well? Or shall we go after new audiences —as dramatization can do better?"

The safest decision may seem, again and again, to talk to those already won. It brings the most wholehearted applause. It avoids friction with producers, writers, technicians and artists who may have ideas of their own. It avoids costly errors. But it may not, in the long run, be the wise decision.

More and more, influence goes to those who reach for new audiences, in the language of all. That language deals in emotions as well as words. The techniques it requires are expensive—so much so, they must generally be used on a national scale.

This brings us to another dilemma, closely related to that of cost.

ORGANIZATION STRUCTURE. In mass communication, the most successful groups have generally been those which comprise (a) a national unit and (b) local units.

Whether technically related, or merely closely allied in purpose, national and local units are essential supplements to each other.

The functions of the national unit include liaison with other national sponsors, producers, distributors; production of materials and programs for nationwide use; fund-raising from national sources.

The functions of the local unit are just as varied, or more so. They may include local fund-raising. The local unit also acts as distributor: served by the films, broadcasts, and press material of the national, it secures their use by local outlets such as stations, newspapers, theaters, schools, clubs, churches. The unit itself also acts as outlet: it arranges discussion groups. It stimulates local action: it helps others find speakers and discussion leaders. It is a local producer: its local broadcasts may be simple in structure but have the advantage of being local; also, they invigorate the organization from the local level. When local units rely entirely on the national for production, a general atrophy may develop. The local also does follow-up research: it may do telephone surveys or other audience studies, during or after broadcasts, and report results to the national. The national, far removed from the local scene, needs this guidance.

Thus each component, national and local, strengthens the other.

An effective combination may be seen in the Anti-Defamation League of B'nai B'rith. The B'nai B'rith lodges created the League to help them perform a special function: the combating of prejudice and discrimination. At first the approach was narrow. It tended to deal with symptoms rather than causes. Protests against stereotypes in art and literature played a part in this approach. Gradually the method widened; it began to emphasize projects done in co-operation with others: various religious, educational, mental health and civil rights groups. The League became less interested in attacking the symptoms of prejudice than in furthering a climate in which the disease could not thrive. The League sponsored productions of a constantly widening subject range; these in turn helped the lodges to establish close ties with a constantly widening range of local groups.

All this helps to explain how the Anti-Defamation League, in 1953, celebrated its fortieth anniversary.

President Eisenhower agreed to accept, at a dinner marking the occasion, the League's Democratic Legacy Award. The League then persuaded Richard Rodgers and Oscar Hammerstein II, foremost theater producers, to stage entertainment for the dinner, to precede the President's acceptance address. It then invited top leaders of government, business and the arts to be present at the dinner. This happened to be a period of tension over civil rights; security measures had led to abuses and angry protests. Would the President exercise leadership toward a reaffirmation of individual rights? The Anti-Defamation League was offering him a platform ideal for this purpose—if he wished to use it. The combination of political tension plus a glittering assembly of notables created a news event of high interest. Television and radio networks agreed to broadcast *Dinner With the President*. Local interest everywhere, aided by local B'nai B'rith promotion, secured acceptance by 140 stations. Seventy-three correspondents, photographers and newsreel men covered the event. Filmed and recorded excerpts ran in theaters, on television and on radio for days afterwards. Distribution of kinescopes, to schools and clubs, continued for weeks.

The President spoke of every man's right to face his accusers. He decried character assassination. It may have been a turning point. His words, on that November 23, 1953, reached about thirty-eight million television viewers, twenty million radio listeners, twenty-five million movie goers, one hundred million newspaper readers. An organization had set it in motion.

We have emphasized that the success of an organization in the mass media may be influenced by its funds, its organizational structure, its choice of techniques.

There is one other factor, already mentioned, that should be emphasized. In most cases, mass communication favors the noncontroversial over the controversial cause. *Dinner With the President* was perhaps an exception. Only the participation of the President made it possible.

Mass communication is a tangle of interrelationships, of free rides. It is an arena in which business, government and organizations often speak in unison, but sometimes do not.

When they speak in unison, they speak with a mighty voice. The matters on which they agree move to the center of national attention. They are magnificently supported.

Matters of disagreement must generally grasp the edges of the mass media.

Mass communication is thus, on the whole, a conservative force. It strengthens what we have.

To call it conservative is to point out a virtue and a danger. To the extent that it conserves what we value and need, it is good. To the extent that it makes us resist change as such, it harbors danger. Since our nation was formed, the capacity for change has been important to us.

Hamilton, Madison and Jay, writing as Publius, were controversial, but this did not keep them from the center of the spotlight. To permeate the communication network of their day, they needed neither funds nor elaborate organization nor dramatization. They sat and wrote letters.

Our communication network is potentially far more powerful. But the power is not as easily used.

"Anyone of you here," said a spokesman of the National Council of Churches at a meeting of religious broadcasters, "can reach with your voice at one time more people than Jesus did in His entire ministry." This was theoretically true. But there is an irony in the truth. Jesus represented a small, unfinanced, controversial minority. Yet standing on a hillside, he could speak to as many as Caesar could.

When the story editor says, "We can't use anything controversial," and says it with a tone of conscious virtue, then there is danger.

4 Sponsor of Sponsors

Business, government, organizations—three kinds of sponsor. We have examined how "they" use the mass media.

Most people are inclined to think of sponsors as "they." A better term might be "we."

The influence of sponsors over the media has been emphasized. It is time to emphasize the public's influence over the sponsors. Most people have no conception of the extent to which sponsors feel dependent on the decisions and whims of the public. To the sponsor, it feels more like this:

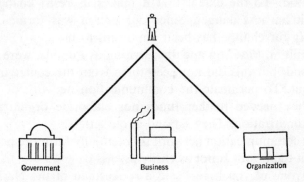

Government   Business   Organization

We the public are, in a very real sense, the sponsor of sponsors.

We endorse or reject the communications of sponsors through a constant series of actions: every time we buy or do not buy an advertised product; every time we vote or do not vote in a local or state or federal election; every time we support or do not support an organization program; every time we read or do not read; listen or do not listen; watch or do not watch.

Constantly, often unknowingly, we participate in the decisions of sponsors. We all share responsibility.

Conscious of this, some people concentrate on attacks and censorship efforts. A more meaningful approach, in the long run, is participation—conscious participation in the decisions of sponsors, whom in any case we influence.

As members of the PTA, we sometimes deplore what we endorse as consumers. As church members, we sometimes champion what we scorn as tuners-in. Again our mass media reflect our inner conflicts, as well as exploiting them.

Our first effort should be to understand the vast, complex organism of mass communication. This is not easy. It calls for better understanding of ourselves. It calls for better understanding of our society.

Next we should try to promote its use, through business, government, and organizations, toward ends in which we believe. This, too, is not easy. But those who accept this view will not draw back from the difficulties, however numerous.

They will not draw back from mass communication because it is huge. They will accept the hugeness as essential, and in itself neither good nor bad.

They will not renounce the mass media because they involve sponsors. The sponsor has always been with us. He, too, seems necessary and is, in himself, neither good nor bad.

They will not draw back in horror from these media because they exert leverage on deep emotional drives. They will accept those drives as the basic raw material of all communication. They will also see those drives as one of our most important resources for tomorrow.

Tension is an ever-present fact of our time. The tension holds great force in check. The work of millions, increasingly mechanized, gives little outlet for that force.

The force is mighty, for good or evil. It can make wars or crusades, filth or beauty. Communication tugs at it, channels it, steers it.

Who will channel it, toward what ends? This is the great question.

It is easy, for those who hold answers for tomorrow, to communicate with each other through the austere narrations of specialized media. Media can build bridges; they can also make walls. With specialized media we can seal ourselves in, reaffirming our rightness.

But the need is for bridges.

BIBLIOGRAPHY: The Sponsors of Mass Communication

SELECTED READINGS

Callahan, Jennie W. *Television in School, College and Community*. New York: McGraw-Hill. 1953.

. Chafee, Zechariah, Jr. *Government and Mass Communications: A Report from the Commission on Freedom of the Press*. 2V. Chicago: University of Chicago Press. 1947.

Cross, H. L. *The People's Right to Know*. New York: Columbia University Press. 1953.

Dale, Edgar. *Audio-Visual Methods in Teaching*. New York: Dryden Press. 1946.

The Dollars and Sense of Business Films. New York: Association of National Advertisers. 1954.

Duffy, Ben. *Advertising Media and Markets*. New York: Prentice-Hall. 1951. (Rev.)

Elliott, Godfrey (ed.). *Film and Education: A Symposium on the*

Role of the Film in the Field of Education. New York: Philosophical Library. 1948.

Film Services of National Associations. Evanston: Film Council of America. 1954.

Frey, Albert Wesley. *Advertising.* New York: Ronald Press. 1947.

Gipson, Henry Clay. *Films in Business and Industry.* New York: McGraw-Hill. 1947.

Hall, Roger S. *Taking Hold of Television: A Guide for Health, Welfare and Civic Organizations.* New York: National Publicity Council. 1954.

How Science Teachers Use Business-Sponsored Teaching Aids. Washington: National Science Teachers Association. 1955.

Lazarsfeld, Paul F.; Berelson, Bernard; and Gaudet, Helen. *The People's Choice.* New York: Columbia University Press. 1948.

Levenson, William B.; and Stasheff, Edward. *Teaching Through Radio and Television.* New York: Rinehart. 1952.

McCamy, James L. *Government Publications for the Citizen.* New York: Columbia University Press. 1950.

————. *Government Publicity: Its Practice in Federal Administration.* Chicago: University of Chicago Press, 1939.

Parker, Everett C.; Barry, David W.; and Smythe, Dallas W. *The Television-Radio Audience and Religion.* New York: Harper. 1955.

Parker, Everett C.; Inman, Elinor; and Snyder, Ross. *Religious Radio: What To Do and How.* New York: Harper. 1948.

Settel, Irving; Glenn, Norman; and associates. *Television Advertising and Production Handbook.* New York: Crowell. 1953.

Shayon, Robert Lewis. *Television and Our Children.* New York: Longmans. 1951.

Starr, Cecile (ed.). *Ideas on Film: A Handbook for the 16 mm Film User.* New York: Funk & Wagnalls. 1951.

Tonkin, Joseph D.; and Skelsi, Alice F. *Television for You: A Handbook for Extension Agents.* Washington: U. S. Department of Agriculture. 1953.

Waldron, Gloria; with Starr, Cecile. *The Information Film.* New York: Columbia University Press. 1949.

Waples, Douglas (ed.). *Print, Radio and Film in a Democracy.* Chicago University of Chicago Press. 1942.

PERIODICALS

Advertising Age. Chicago.

Audio-Visual Guide. Maplewood, N. J.

Business Screen Magazine. Chicago.

The Christian Broadcaster. New York: National Council of Churches.

Educational Screen. Chicago.

Film News. New York: Sairlee Enterprises.

Film World. Hollywood.

Journal of the AERT. Chicago: Association for Education by Radio-Television.

See and Hear. Chicago.

Sponsor. New York.

Tide. New York: Billboard Publishing Company.

REFERENCE WORKS

(Issued periodically, unless date is given)

Directory of Non-Royalty Films for Television. Ames: Iowa State College Press. 1954.

Educational Film Guide. New York: H. W. Wilson.

TV Dictionary and Handbook for Sponsors. New York: Sponsor Magazine. 1955.

U. S. Government Films for Television. Washington: U. S. Office of Education.

INDEX

273